FOLLOWING IN THE FOOTSTEPS
OF
EDWARD II

FOLLOWING IN THE FOOTSTEPS OF
EDWARD II

A HISTORICAL GUIDE TO THE MEDIEVAL KING

KATHRYN WARNER

PEN & SWORD **HISTORY**

AN IMPRINT OF PEN & SWORD BOOKS LTD.
YORKSHIRE – PHILADELPHIA

First published in Great Britain in 2019 by
Pen and Sword History
An imprint of
Pen & Sword Books Ltd
Yorkshire - Philadelphia

ISBN 978 1 52673 293 4

Typeset in Ehrhardt MT Std 11.5/14 by
Aura Technology and Software Services, India

Printed and bound in UK by TJ International Ltd.

Pen & Sword Books Ltd incorporates the Imprints of Pen & Sword Books
Archaeology, Atlas, Aviation, Battleground, Discovery, Family History, History,
Maritime, Military, Naval, Politics, Railways, Select, Transport, True Crime,
Fiction, Frontline Books, Leo Cooper, Praetorian Press, Seaforth Publishing,
Wharncliffe and White Owl.

For a complete list of Pen & Sword titles please contact

PEN & SWORD BOOKS LIMITED
47 Church Street, Barnsley, South Yorkshire, S70 2AS, England
E-mail: enquiries@pen-and-sword.co.uk
Website: www.pen-and-sword.co.uk

or

PEN AND SWORD BOOKS
1950 Lawrence Rd, Havertown, PA 19083, USA
E-mail: Uspen-and-sword@casematepublishers.com
Website: www.penandswordbooks.com

Contents

Introduction

Edward II (born 1284, reigned 1307–27) is famously one of England's most unsuccessful kings, as utterly different from his domineering father Edward I (r. 1272–1307) and his warrior son Edward III (r. 1327–77) as any man possibly could be. Highly unconventional, even eccentric, his was an intriguing personality, and his reign of nineteen-and-a-half years from July 1307 to January 1327 was a turbulent period which saw endless conflict and wars with his own barons, and the king's infatuation with a parade of men. His reign ended catastrophically after his own queen Isabella of France (c. 1295–1358) led an invasion of his kingdom in September 1326. Edward's support collapsed within a few weeks, and he was forced to abdicate his throne to his 14-year-old son Edward III in January 1327, the first time this happened in English history. *Following in the Footsteps of Edward II* presents a new take on this most eccentric and puzzling of kings, telling his story from the perspective of the places in Britain which mattered most in his life, such as the magnificent Caernarfon Castle where he was born in 1284 shortly after his father conquered North Wales, his favourite residence at Kings Langley in Hertfordshire, the battlefield of Bannockburn near Stirling in Scotland where he led an army to the greatest military defeat in English history, the castle of Berkeley in Gloucestershire where he supposedly met his brutal death in September 1327, and Gloucester Cathedral, where his tomb and alabaster effigy still exist and are among the greatest glories surviving from medieval England.

Chapter One

King in Waiting, 1284–1307

Caernarfon Castle, Gwynedd, North Wales: Edward's Birthplace

It is entirely possible that a king of England was born in the middle of a muddy building site. In the North Wales town of Caernarfon on the feast day of Saint Mark the Evangelist in the twelfth year of her husband's reign, or Tuesday, 25 April 1284 as we call it, the Spanish queen of England gave birth to at least her fourteenth, and perhaps her fifteenth or sixteenth, child. Leonor or Eleanor of Castile was now about 42 years old, and this would be her last delivery. She died in November 1290 when she was 49 years old and her youngest child only 6, and of the fourteen or more children she had borne, only six outlived her: daughters Eleanor, Joan of Acre, Margaret, Mary and Elizabeth, and Edward of Caernarfon, the youngest. Edward, later King Edward II, was the first of only two English monarchs in history with a Spanish parent (the second was Mary Tudor, born in 1516 as the daughter of Henry VIII and Katherine of Aragon), and the first of three to be born in Wales (the others were Henry V in 1386 and Henry VII in 1457).

Both of Edward of Caernarfon's grandmothers, Eleanor of Provence and Jeanne of Ponthieu, were French, and by blood he was more French than anything else, partly Spanish, and only minimally English. Only one of his eight great-grandparents (King John) was even born in England, and not one of his sixteen great-great-grandparents. Edward's mother, Queen Leonor, gave birth to a large family, and had also been born into one; she was the twelfth of the fifteen children of the great warrior king Fernando III, ruler of Castile and Leon, two of the four kingdoms of

1

medieval Spain. Edward II's maternal grandfather (b. 1201, r. 1217–52) was made a saint of the Catholic Church in 1671, as San Fernando or Saint Ferdinand. The saintly warrior played a hugely important role in the centuries-long *Reconquista*, the 'Reconquest' of the Iberian Peninsula from its Muslim rulers, and is now the patron saint of Seville, the city in southern Spain he captured from the Almohad caliphate in 1248 after more than 500 years of Muslim rule. Fernando's daughter Leonor was only 10 when he died in Seville in May 1252, and two-and-a-half years later married the heir to the English throne, Lord Edward (b. 1239), at Burgos in northern Spain. Lord Edward and Doña Leonor succeeded as king and queen of England in November 1272, on the death of Edward's father Henry III. Their youngest child Edward of Caernarfon was born a few months short of thirty years after their wedding.

Edward of Caernarfon's father Edward I invaded North Wales in 1282, and its last native ruler, Llywelyn ap Gruffudd, was killed in an ambush in December that year. The birth of the king of England's latest child in Caernarfon was intended as propaganda to hammer home the message of his conquest of Gwynedd and his subjugation of its people (though the often-repeated story that the king promised to give the inhabitants of Gwynedd a prince who spoke no English, then sneakily presented them with his new-born son Edward of Caernarfon, is an invention of 300 years later). Edward I's fifth surviving daughter Elizabeth had been born in the North Wales town of Rhuddlan in August 1282, also an attempt to have the potential heir to the English throne born in Wales, which failed when the child was a girl. The boy born in Caernarfon in April 1284 was not, however, the direct heir to the English throne at the time of his birth; that was his 10-year-old brother Alfonso, born in Bayonne in south-west France in November 1273. He was named after his uncle and godfather King Alfonso X of Castile and Leon (r. 1252–84), the eldest of Queen Leonor's eleven brothers and half-brothers. Alfonso of Bayonne died suddenly on 19 August 1284, whereupon his 4-month-old brother Edward of Caernarfon became heir to the throne. From 1274 to 1284, the English people had grown used to the idea that one day they would have a king called Alfonso of Bayonne; sadly it was not to be. Two other sons of Edward I and Queen Leonor, John and Henry, also died in childhood in 1271 and 1274, long before their little brother Edward of Caernarfon was born.

A fortification on the castle site at Caernarfon had existed since Roman times, and the Normans built a motte and bailey castle there in the early 1100s. Beginning c. May 1283, Edward I had whatever still existed on the site knocked down and began the construction of his massive stone castle, one of his chain of great strongholds stretching across North Wales: Caernarfon, Rhuddlan, Conwy, Beaumaris and Harlech. In April 1284 at the time of Edward II's birth, the castle, which still stands in Caernarfon, was in the earliest stages of construction. It therefore perhaps seems unlikely that the room on an upper floor of the Eagle Tower pointed out to visitors today as the birthplace of Edward II had already been built. Then again, the Eagle Tower is the oldest part of the castle and work on it, and on the town and the town walls, did progress very rapidly in the 1280s. Leonor of Castile may have given birth to her son in whatever had already been built of the Eagle Tower by April 1284, or in a temporary timber building on the site, or perhaps she had decided to take lodgings somewhere in the town itself which Edward I was having built at the same time. The exact location of Edward II's birthplace is, therefore, not entirely certain. In his own lifetime and afterwards, and indeed even today, Edward was strongly associated with the town of his birth. In January 1330, over two years after Edward's reported death at Berkeley Castle, his friend the Archbishop of York referred to him in a letter to the mayor of London as 'our liege lord Edward of Caernarfon' (he spelt Caernarfon as 'Karnarvan'), and in the 1350s one chronicler even called Edward's wife Isabella of France 'Lady Isabella of Caernarfon'.

Edward was christened in Caernarfon on 1 May 1284, and his first wet-nurse was a woman of the town called Mariota Maunsel, to whom he granted an annual income of £5 twenty-three years later in 1307 after he became king. The boy left Caernarfon and Wales in the summer of 1284 when he was only a few months old – although he travelled to Wales a few years later, he was never again to set foot in his birthplace – while work continued on his father's new castle and would do so for several decades. Caernarfon Castle was intended as a symbol of the English king's dominance of Wales and of the Welsh people. In September 1294 when Edward of Caernarfon was 10 years old, the Welsh nobleman Madog ap Llywelyn led a revolt against Edward I, and burned some of Caernarfon Castle and the town walls. This rebellion was put down in 1295 by the wealthy and powerful Gilbert 'the Red' de Clare, earl of Gloucester and Hertford (b. 1243), who, rather oddly, was Edward of Caernarfon's brother-in-law although he was forty years the boy's senior; Gloucester married Edward's older sister Joan of Acre (b. 1272) in 1290.

William Beauchamp, earl of Warwick (c. 1240–98), also took part in putting down Madog's rebellion. Warwick's grandson Hugh Despenser the Younger, born in the late 1280s and a young child at the time of the Welsh rebellion, would later marry Edward II's eldest niece, and would become Edward's powerful and despotic favourite in the 1320s. Other than Madog ap Llywelyn's rebellion, Caernarfon Castle never saw military action, except when it was besieged again in 1400 during the revolt of the Welsh nobleman Owain Glyn Dŵr (whose name is sometimes anglicised as 'Owen Glendower'), early in the reign of Edward II's great-grandson Henry IV (r. 1399–1413).

Caernarfon Castle stands looking over the southern end of the Menai Strait which divides the mainland of North Wales from the island of Anglesey, and was built in that location to control Edward I's access to the rich and fertile island which was called 'the garden of Wales'. Between 1283 and 1292, Edward I spent the huge sum of £13,000 on the castle, the equivalent of many millions of pounds today. The king never saw his great castle completed; his son Edward II continued the work at Caernarfon throughout his reign, and it was not until 1330, early in the reign of Edward II's son, Edward III (r. 1327–77), that the castle was completed (and even then, some of the planned buildings in the inner ward were never constructed). Even today, the entire town of Caernarfon stands within the castle walls – the circuit measures 800 yards – and the castle itself, with its seven polygonal towers and walls 20ft thick, looks as dominating, daunting and massive as it must have appeared 700 years ago. A stone statue of Edward II which dates to around 1320 when he was 34 years old still stands on the exterior of the King's Gate of the castle, though as Edward did not visit Caernarfon again after he was born there in 1284, he never saw it, nor had any chance to spend time in one of the four luxurious towers built to accommodate the royal family and their guests. These were the King's and Queen's Towers, the Chamberlain Tower, and the Black Tower. Edward I made his son and heir Prince of Wales in February 1301, and it may be that he had it in mind for his son and the young man's household to live at Caernarfon at least some of the time, but this never happened, perhaps because the king spent much of the last years of his reign fighting in Scotland and took his son with him.

Caernarfon Castle is now looked after by Cadw, the historic environment service of the Welsh government, and is, with Beaumaris Castle,

Harlech Castle and Conwy Castle, part of, 'The Castles and Town Walls of King Edward in Gwynedd.' This has been a UNESCO-designated World Heritage Site since 1986. Caernarfon Castle is open to the public daily except on 24, 25 and 26 December and 1 January, and entrance costs a few pounds; under-5s can visit for free and there is a discount for under-16s, senior citizens and students. Cadw also offers annual or lifelong membership with free entrance to its properties, and three- and seven-day Explorer Passes for visitors to Wales. The town of Caernarfon is easily reached by car or bus from the A487, 9 miles from Bangor; Bangor is also the nearest main line railway station. Caernarfon is one of the most impressive castles in Britain, even in Europe; a visit is an absolute must.

Conwy Castle, Conwy County Borough, North Wales: Edward, the New Prince of Wales

Edward of Caernarfon finally returned to Wales when he was 17 years old in the spring of 1301, after his father gave him the principality of Wales and the earldom of Chester (see below under 'Lincoln Cathedral'). A few weeks after the ceremony which bestowed these lands on him on 7 February 1301, Edward, bearing the proud title 'Prince of Wales', travelled to North Wales to take the homage of his Welsh vassals. He stayed at Conwy Castle from 28 April until 5 May 1301, a few days after his seventeenth birthday.

Conwy Castle was built by Edward I between 1283 and 1289, and the king also built the town's walls which encircle Conwy to this day and measure 800 yards in total length. The same architect, Master James St George, worked on both Caernarfon and Conwy, and Edward I's outlay on Conwy was even greater than on Caernarfon. It was built on a rock base, a natural fortification, and still has eight towers. Accommodation at Conwy was, by the standards of the time, luxurious, and there were royal chambers and a chapel in the inner ward where Edward of Caernarfon must have stayed and worshipped in 1301. He must have known that his father had briefly been besieged at Conwy in December 1294, during the rebellion of Madog ap Llewelyn. A famous story related by a chronicler called Walter of Guisborough relates how Edward I refused to drink his own personal supply of wine at this time, but insisted that it should be shared among the Conwy garrison.

After 1301, Edward II never visited North Wales or Conwy Castle again. On 30 January 1326, just under a year before his forced deposition, he appointed the noblewoman Alina, Lady Burnell, née Despenser (c. 1287–1363) as the constable of Conwy Castle. This was a rare honour; Alina was only the second woman in the fourteenth century, after Edward II's second cousin Isabella, Lady Vescy, née Beaumont at Bamburgh in 1304 and again in 1307, to be put in charge of a castle. Alina's appointment probably came as a result of the influence of her brother Hugh Despenser the Younger (c. 1288/89–1326), who from 1319 until his execution in 1326, was Edward II's chamberlain and mighty 'favourite'. Edward II's great-grandson Richard II (r. 1377–99) spent time at Conwy Castle in 1399 shortly before he surrendered to his cousin Henry of Lancaster, who was soon to take the throne as Henry IV, and in March 1401 Conwy fell during the revolt of Owain Glyn Dŵr. The castle saw action again in the 1640s, during the Civil War.

The wall walks built by Edward I in the 1280s survive almost intact and still encircle the town, and it is possible to walk much of the way around the town on the walls (though some parts are not safe). For information on visiting Conwy, see above, under the entry for Caernarfon Castle. Conwy is about 23 miles from Caernarfon, and the town has its own railway station. Like Caernarfon, Conwy is one of the great castles of medieval Europe, and a must-see.

Kings Langley, Hertfordshire: Edward's Favourite Residence

Edward of Caernarfon's childhood was peripatetic, something he had in common with all royals and all great noblemen and noblewomen of the Middle Ages, and he and his household spent a large part of the year travelling around the south and Midlands of England. There is much evidence, though, to suggest that both in childhood and in adulthood Edward II's favourite residence was the palace of Langley in Hertfordshire, and he spent much time there. The town became known as Kings Langley later in the Middle Ages because of its association with Edward II and his royal successors, though in Edward's own lifetime was often called 'Childerlangley' or simply 'Langley'. Edward, then aged 24, founded a Dominican priory at Langley in December 1308 'in fulfilment of a vow

6

made by the king in peril'. The Dominicans were, and are still, known as the Blackfriars or the Friars Preacher, and were founded by Saint Dominic in 1216; Edward II supported the order staunchly, and they reciprocated and were among his most loyal followers throughout his reign and even afterwards. All Edward's confessors were Dominican friars, and some of his tutors in childhood were also Dominicans.

On 20 December 1308, Edward granted the Dominican order £100 annually and gave them his 'garden adjacent to the parish church of that place [Langley], with two plots of land next to the garden'. The friary was built in Edward's park at Langley, and he also gave the friars his building of 'Little London' at Langley for them to live in while the new priory was built. By 1312, forty-five friars lived at Langley. At the beginning of 1315, Edward had his beloved friend and companion, perhaps lover, Piers Gaveston, earl of Cornwall, buried at Langley Priory, and spent large sums of money on the funeral, on Piers' tomb in later years, and on praying for Gaveston's soul for many years after his death. Gaveston was killed in Warwickshire on 19 June 1312 (see under 'Warwick Castle' below); Edward, morbidly, refused to bury him until two-and-a-half years after his death, and the embalmed body remained with the Dominican friars of Oxford.

Edward II also attempted to found a house of nuns at Langley in the late 1310s and 1320s, but his plans floundered. His son Edward III, however, took an interest in his father's foundation, and in 1349 finally established a house of Benedictine nuns at Langley. The priory was closed down during the Dissolution in the sixteenth century, though Henry VIII's daughter Mary Tudor and her husband Philip II of Spain re-founded Langley in 1557 as a house of Dominican nuns. Its second lifespan was very short; it was closed down again shortly after Mary's half-sister Elizabeth I succeeded her to the throne in November 1558.

Edward II's palace of Langley on Langley Hill originally belonged to his mother, Leonor of Castile, who acquired it in 1276, and records show that Edward's older brother Alfonso of Bayonne (1273–84), his parents' third son, had his own chamber at Langley. Queen Leonor died in November 1290 and Langley passed to her husband Edward I. In 1302, the king granted it outright to his 18-year-old son Edward of Caernarfon, then Prince of Wales, earl of Chester and count of Ponthieu, who had already spent much of his childhood at the palace. Edward stayed there from November 1292 until April 1293, when he was 8 years old, and on numerous other occasions. In 1292, the great hall of Langley was whitewashed and the walls painted in vivid yellow and vermilion; a mural of four knights attending a jousting tournament was painted on one wall. This gives some idea of the kind of interior decoration Edward grew up with and was used to.

All his life, Edward II showed a great interest in the outdoors and in taking part in vigorous physical exercise; in childhood he was, unlike his three older brothers who all died young, a sturdy, healthy boy. He must have explored the meadows, pastures and 8 acres of parkland surrounding his palace at Langley, and the great interest he showed later in life in what his detractors sneered at as 'rustic pursuits' unsuitable for the heir to the throne must have developed when he lived there. One chronicler stated: 'from his youth he [Edward] devoted himself in private to the art of rowing and driving carts, of digging ditches and thatching houses...and to other pointless trivial occupations unsuitable for the son of a king.' There is ample evidence from the 1320s that Edward went fishing, spent time watching others fishing, and chatting to fishermen and women; he dug ditches, thatched roofs and enjoyed metalwork. He also enjoyed swimming and rowing, even in winter. Although nowadays Edward's love of the outdoors and physical exercise would doubtless make him an excellent role model for a nation with an increasingly sedentary lifestyle, his contemporaries reacted to his fondness for digging, thatching, rowing, fishing and metalwork with scathing criticism, because kings were simply not meant to perform such tasks. Edward II was, in many ways, born out of his time; his fondness for spending time with his common subjects, which nowadays might cause him to be applauded as a king with the common touch, also attracted withering criticism from chroniclers. To give just a handful of examples, Edward went on holiday in 1315 with a 'great company of common people'; had a friend in the 1320s called Colle Herron, a Thames fisherman; invited shipwrights to come and stay with him, and dined with a group of carpenters. He also had a fondness for sailing along the River Thames near London and chatting to the fishermen and fisherwomen he encountered along the river; it seems almost certain that he behaved in the same way when he was growing up at Kings Langley.

Kings Langley lies on the River Gade about 20 miles north-west of central London, and 2 miles from both Watford and Hemel Hempstead.

The site of the medieval palace is a scheduled ancient monument, though sadly little exists of it today except some archaeological remains. The palace Edward II inherited was built around three courtyards and had a moat, a large wine cellar, a bath-house, a large chamber for Edward with a fireplace, and a paved cloister for the queen. A huge wine cellar was built in the early 1290s, and there was a bakehouse and a place called 'le Longrewe' or 'long room'. Queen Leonor spent two years developing a garden at her palace of Langley, in which fruit trees and vines grew, and employed gardeners from Aragon, one of the four Spanish kingdoms. Her son Edward kept his pet camel there, and also a lion (though sometimes took the lion with him on a silver chain as he travelled around England). He stayed at Langley numerous times throughout his reign, including in May/June 1308; shortly before Christmas 1308; the first four months of 1309; much of June to September 1309; Easter 1323, and Easter 1324.

Edward's grandson, Edmund of Langley, first duke of York and the fourth son of Edward III, was born at the palace of Langley on 5 June 1341, and died there sixty-one years later; he and his first wife Isabel of Castile (c. 1355–92) were both buried at Langley Priory. Edmund's nephew, Edward II's great-grandson Richard II, was originally buried at Langley Priory, Edward II's foundation, after he was murdered at Pontefract Castle in Yorkshire on or about 14 February 1400. After Henry V's accession to the throne in 1413, however, he had Richard's remains moved to Westminster Abbey to lie next to his queen, Anne of Bohemia (1366–94). Most of the tombs inside Langley Priory were lost at the Dissolution in the sixteenth century, including Edward II's companion Piers Gaveston, but those of Edmund of Langley and his wife Isabel of Castile were moved into All Saints Church in the town later in the sixteenth century, and can still be seen there. Edward II would recognise parts of All Saints, as they date from the thirteenth century.

A Rudolf Steiner school stood on the site of Edward II's palace at Kings Langley but was closed down in July 2017; some ruined walls and fragments of stonework still exist of his palace and are Grade II Listed. One of the buildings of the priory founded by Edward in 1308 is also still extant and stands in what was the grounds of the Rudolf Steiner school, and the name of the Old Palace pub on Langley Hill commemorates Edward II's home.

Caerlaverock Castle, Dumfries and Galloway, Scotland: Edward's First Military Encounter

In July 1300, Edward I besieged Caerlaverock Castle during one of his frequent military campaigns in Scotland, and his son and heir Edward of Caernarfon took part. The siege took place two years after the king's victory over the Scots at the battle of Falkirk and three years after his defeat to the famous Sir William Wallace, star of the Hollywood blockbuster *Braveheart*, at the battle of Stirling Bridge. Edward I's brother-in-law, King Alexander III of Scotland, had died in March 1286 when he rode his horse off an embankment during a storm, and was found the next morning with a broken neck. Alexander's three children (whose mother was Edward I's sister Margaret of England) were all already dead, and his only heir was his toddler granddaughter Margaret of Norway, daughter of King Erik II of Norway and Alexander's daughter Margaret of Scotland. Edward I betrothed Margaret of Norway, his great-niece, to his son Edward of Caernarfon in 1289 when she was 6 and he 5. One day this marriage would have made Edward II king of Scotland as well as king of England, Prince of Wales and lord of Ireland, but his little fiancée died at the age of 7 in September 1290 without ever setting foot in her kingdom. Alexander III's line had run out, and over 100 adjudicators, with Edward I of England at their head, were appointed to assess the claims of a dozen men to the Scottish throne. They chose John Balliol, and he was crowned king of Scotland in 1292, but in 1296 allied with Philip IV of France against Edward I, and Edward invaded Scotland and removed Balliol from the throne. For ten years there was an interregnum in Scotland.

As his fee for adjudicating the matter of its rightful king, Edward I had claimed the right to be overlord of Scotland, and declared that the Scottish kings held their kingdom from him and owed him fealty for it. In the late 1290s and early 1300s, he often fought in Scotland, and bequeathed a war there to his son on his death in July 1307. Among the factors which led ultimately to Edward II's deposition in 1327 were his failures in Scotland and his inability to defeat its king, Robert Bruce (r. 1306–29); Bruce killed Edward's great rival John 'the Red Comyn' in February 1306 and had himself crowned king of Scotland soon afterwards.

Three thousand men-at-arms and no fewer than eighty-seven members of the English nobility joined King Edward I on his Scottish campaign of

1300 which was intended to subdue resistance to him in the south-west of Scotland. One of them was the king's 16-year-old son and heir, Edward, taking part in his first military engagement.

The English heralds wrote a long and extremely flattering ode to the English noblemen who participated in the siege of Caerlaverock, in French (or rather Anglo-Norman, the variant of French used by the medieval English nobility). They called Edward of Caernarfon, 'a well-proportioned and handsome person, of a courteous disposition, and intelligent, and desirous of finding an occasion to display his prowess. He managed his steed wonderfully well.' His name appears in the poem as 'Edewars', and despite his youth he was in command of the 'fourth squadron'. Edward's first cousins John of Brittany (b. c. 1266), and the two Lancaster brothers (b. c. 1277/8 and 1280/81), also took part in the siege. The heralds called the Lancasters, 'two brothers, cousins to the king's son, named Thomas and Henry, who were the sons of Lord Edmund, the well-beloved.' John of Brittany spent most of his life in England and was known by the nickname 'Brito', was called 'handsome and gentle' by the writers of the poem. One of the heralds perhaps had something of a crush on the 26-year-old Robert, Lord Clifford (who was destined to fall fighting for Edward II at the battle of Bannockburn fourteen years later), declaring: 'If I were a maiden, I would give him my heart and body, so good is his fame,' and, 'I well know that I have given him no praise of which he is not worthy. For he exhibits as good proofs of wisdom and prudence as any I see.' The 33-year-old earl of Arundel, Richard Fitzalan, also came in for praise for his good looks, being described as 'a handsome and well-loved knight'. Edward I himself was called, 'dreadful, fierce and proud; for none experience his bite who are not poisoned by it.' Edward of Caernarfon was one who was poisoned by his father's bite on two occasions, in 1305 and 1307 (see below under 'Lanercost Priory').

In the end, the siege of Caerlaverock in July 1300 proved something of an anti-climax, and the large force taken by Edward I was probably overkill, given that the castle had not really been designed to withstand an all-out assault on it. The small garrison attacked the English forces with stones and arrows, but were forced to surrender after only a few days. Edward I and his host carried on deeper into Scotland to continue the campaign, and for the remaining seven years of his life the old king did not go near Caerlaverock again. (The castle was besieged for a second time

11

340 years later in 1640, during the Civil War.) Edward II also did not see Caerlaverock again after the siege of 1300, though in early August 1307 he passed nearby, shortly after his father's death and his own accession to the throne, when he travelled from Carlisle to Dumfries.

Caerlaverock Castle is well worth a visit, being of a curious and unique triangular shape; the red sandstone building and its wide moat are picturesque. Much of the medieval castle survives, and it is a popular location for filming as well as a tourist attraction. The English heralds who described the siege of Caerlaverock in 1300 were also impressed at what they saw: 'It was formed like a shield, for it had only three sides in circuit, with a tower at each angle ... I believe you will never see a castle more beautifully situated.'

Caerlaverock is 8 miles south of Dumfries and 30 miles west of Carlisle over the English border, and stands at the edge of the Solway Firth. The organisation Historic Scotland now looks after the castle, which is open every day of the year except 25 and 26 December and 1 January. Lochmaben Castle, just 11 miles from Caerlaverock, was the birthplace in 1307 of Edward II's nephew Humphrey de Bohun, earl of Hereford and Essex, second eldest surviving son of Edward's sister Elizabeth of Rhuddlan (1282–1316). Humphrey succeeded his elder brother John as earl of Hereford in 1336, and died in 1361. Lochmaben was built by the English in the early 1300s, soon after the siege of Caerlaverock Castle, as an outpost in Scotland, and is now ruins in woodland next to a loch. Eight miles from Caerlaverock is the 5-metre high Ruthwell Cross, which dates to the early 700s AD. Lines of poetry on the cross, in both the Latin alphabet and the ancient runic alphabet, show a striking similarity to the famous Old English poem *The Dream of the Rood*.

Lincoln Cathedral and Chapter-House, Lincolnshire: Edward Becomes Prince of Wales

For 238 years from 1311 (in Edward II's reign) until 1549, when its central spire collapsed, Lincoln Cathedral was the tallest building in the known world. Edward II held parliament here from 27 January until 23 February 1316, and also visited the cathedral in April 1314 a few weeks before his defeat at the battle of Bannockburn in Scotland, in October 1314, and again in August 1317.

Work began on Lincoln Cathedral in 1072 on the orders of Remigius, then Bishop of Lincoln, and continued into the fifteenth century, though a fire in 1124 and an earthquake in 1185 both partially destroyed it. The chapter-house was built between 1220 and 1235, and it was here that Edward II held parliament in early 1316. The octagonal room is still used as a venue for concerts and other events.

A very important event in the future King Edward II's life took place in the chapter-house of Lincoln Cathedral on 7 February 1301, when he was 16 going on 17. His father bestowed the principality of Wales and the earldom of Chester on him. Edward of Caernarfon was the first heir to the English throne to be made Prince of Wales and earl of Chester, and more than 700 years later in the twenty-first century, the tradition continues. Edward II did not make his own son Edward of Windsor (the future Edward III) Prince of Wales, perhaps considering the boy too young, though he did make him earl of Chester when his son was only a few days old in November 1312. The next Prince of Wales after Edward II was, therefore, his grandson Edward of Woodstock, born in June 1330 as Edward III's eldest son, followed by Edward of Woodstock's son Richard of Bordeaux (b. 1367), the future King Richard II of England. Before 1301, the princes of Wales were the native rulers of the principality. Llywelyn ap Gruffudd, the last true Prince of Wales, was killed in December 1282 during Edward I's invasion of his lands. His brother Dafydd ap Gruffudd, though technically the last native Prince of Wales, never ruled and suffered the traitor's death on the orders of Edward I in Shrewsbury on 3 October 1283, six-and-a-half months before Edward of Caernarfon's birth.

Edward II's parliament at Lincoln between 27 January and 20 February 1316 occurred during a terrible period of European history. In 1314, 1315 and into 1316, it barely stopped raining in northern Europe, with the result that crops failed everywhere and up to 10 per cent of the population starved to death or died of disease. This tragic period from 1315 to 1317 is now known as the Great Famine (see also below under 'Berwick-upon-Tweed'). While at Lincoln in early 1316, Edward II tried to alleviate the suffering of his starving subjects by fixing the prices of basic foodstuffs so that they remained affordable; scarcity had driven prices up to unmanageable levels, so that, for example, two small onions at Cheapside in London cost a penny, which was an entire day's wages for many people. The king declared that a 'fat sheep' should cost no more than 20*d* if unshorn and 14*d* if shorn; a 'live fat cow' no more than 12*s*; a fat chicken, 1½*d*; two dozen eggs, 1*d*. He also ordered his nobles to limit the number of courses they consumed at their dinner tables. Unfortunately for the people of England and Wales, the Great Famine occurred during a difficult phase in politics when Edward II's powerful cousin and enemy Thomas, earl of Lancaster, was appointed as the king's chief counsellor, but such was the hostility between the two men that they could not work or cooperate together. In effect, the cousins' rivalry left England more or less ungoverned during the worst natural disaster of the early fourteenth century.

Lincoln Cathedral had a family connection to Edward II: his mother Leonor of Castile died in Harby 7 miles from Lincoln on 28 November 1290, and although most of her body was buried at Westminster Abbey on 17 December, her entrails were buried in Lincoln Cathedral. (Her heart was given to the Dominican friars of London.) Edward was just 6 years old when he lost his Spanish mother, and as she had spent more than three years of his childhood outside England he cannot have spent much time with her or known her very well, but he punctiliously marked the anniversary of her death every year. Leonor's grieving widower Edward I, to whom she had been married for thirty-six of her forty-nine years, built the famous memorials called the Eleanor Crosses for his wife. One of them stood in Lincoln and part of it still exists inside the grounds of Lincoln Castle. Inside Lincoln Cathedral, Edward I placed a tomb which contained his wife's viscera and was a replica of her tomb in Westminster Abbey. The original stone chest of the Lincoln tomb still exists, though the effigy of Leonor on top of it was destroyed in the seventeenth century, and a copy was made in the nineteenth. When Edward II held parliament inside Lincoln Cathedral in early 1316, and visited the city again eighteen months later, he surely took the time to pray at his mother's tomb there, and to gaze at her effigy.

Lincoln Cathedral is located in the centre of the city of Lincoln, three minutes' walk from the remains of Lincoln Castle. Within the castle grounds, inside the gatehouse, is the oriel window which is all that remains of a wealthy merchant's house dating from the late fourteenth century. Edward II's grandson John of Gaunt, duke of Lancaster (1340–99), is believed to have stayed in this house during his visit to Lincoln in 1386. The cathedral cloisters were built in 1295, in Edward II's childhood, and in 1311, four years into his reign, the central tower was completed; it was 3ft higher than the Great Pyramid at Giza.

The city of Lincoln has a long history. Founded by the Romans around 48 AD, it was the location of two famous medieval battles. The first was fought in 1141 during the Anarchy when King Stephen (r. 1135–54) and his cousin the Empress Maud (1102–67) battled over the English throne; the second battle came early in the reign of Edward II's grandfather Henry III (b. 1207, r. 1216–72) in 1217. On this occasion, the royalist baron William Marshal, earl of Pembroke, defeated the forces of Louis of France, who had invaded England the year before at the invitation of some of King John's (r. 1199–1216) disgruntled barons. Louis subsequently withdrew to France. As well as the cathedral and the castle, another famous tourist attraction in Lincoln is the Jew's House, dating to around 1160 and one of the oldest surviving houses in England, currently a restaurant. The Jew's House stands on the aptly-named Steep Hill a few minutes' walk from the cathedral, and Edward II would have known it.

Lincoln is, at least by English standards, a rather remote city, though it does have its own railway station. The cathedral is open to the public every day, and guided tours are available.

Lanercost Priory, Cumbria: Edward's Quarrel with his Father

Edward I stayed at Lanercost Priory in the far north-west corner of his kingdom for the entire period from 2 October 1306 until 4 March 1307. On 7 July 1307, the king, then 68 years old, died at Burgh-by-Sands 17 miles away. His 22-year-old son Edward stayed at Lanercost Priory with his father and stepmother Queen Marguerite, who became the second wife of Edward I in 1299.

There is much evidence that Edward of Caernarfon loved staying in religious houses and talking to men of religion. In 1300 before the campaign to Scotland and the siege of Caerlaverock, Edward I and his son had spent some days at the Benedictine abbey of Bury St Edmunds in Suffolk. According to the abbey chronicler, Edward of Caernarfon stayed on for a few days after his father left because it pleased him greatly to be there, and took his meals daily in the refectory with the brethren.

While the king and his son were at Lanercost Priory in December 1306, they received a visit from a papal nuncio called Pedro, Castilian by birth and cardinal-bishop of Santa Sabina. Pedro had, reportedly, come to England with a remarkable proposition. Edward of Caernarfon's first cousin once removed, King Fernando IV of Castile and Leon (r. 1295–1312), had been married to Constança of Portugal for some years but had not yet fathered a child. According to a contemporary newsletter, Cardinal Pedro had entered into an indenture with the magnates of Castile that Edward, as the son of King Fernando III's daughter Leonor, would succeed as king of Castile should Fernando IV die without a male heir. Fernando, as it happened, finally fathered a son in 1311 after ten years of marriage; the future King Alfonso XI (whom Edward II betrothed to his daughter Eleanor of Woodstock in 1324, while Alfonso's sister Leonor was betrothed to Edward's son, the future Edward III). Edward I remarked to Cardinal Pedro while at Lanercost Priory in late 1306 that, 'he should have a special affection for our dear son Edward, as he [Edward] is of Spanish descent.' Edward of Caernarfon's uncle Don Enrique, one of his mother's eleven brothers and half-brothers, had suggested in 1303 that Edward should marry Fernando IV's sister, Isabel of Castile. The young man's betrothal to Isabella of France, however, arranged in 1299, could not be broken because the English kings would lose control of their large territories in France forever. Edward of Caernarfon, being half-Castilian himself, might have preferred to marry a Castilian bride rather than a French one, but the decision was out of his hands. In the 1320s, he betrothed three of his and Isabella of France's four children into Spain, and his letters to the royal family of Castile reveal the 'joy' (his own word) he felt at the prospect of his daughter Eleanor of Woodstock becoming the queen of his own mother Leonor's homeland. (In the end, owing to Edward's deposition in early 1327, none of the marriages he had planned for his children took place, and his daughter Eleanor ultimately married the duke of Guelders in the modern-day Netherlands in 1332.)

Lanercost Priory in early 1307 was also the scene of a terrible quarrel between Edward I and his son and heir which came to the attention of chroniclers. Arguably the most important person in Edward of Caernarfon's life, bar none, was Piers Gaveston, a young man he met in the late 1290s and seemingly fell deeply in love with. Gaveston was murdered by some of Edward's magnates in 1312, and Edward remembered him for the rest of his life: among numerous other examples, he had prayers said for Gaveston's soul in June 1326 in the last year of his reign, fourteen years after Gaveston's death. The precise nature of Edward's relationship with Piers Gaveston cannot be determined for certain, though it seems almost beyond doubt that the two men were lovers.

Gaveston was a nobleman from Béarn in the very far south-west of France, in the foothills of the Pyrenees near the Spanish border, and arrived in England with his father Arnaud in 1297. The part of France where he grew up was ruled by the English kings in the Middle Ages, hence it is not really accurate to call Gaveston 'French'; he was a subject of the English crown, and although some later writers, and even some fourteenth-century chroniclers, believed he was a low-born nobody, his father and grandfathers were among the leading barons of Béarn. In or before 1300, Edward I placed Piers Gaveston in his son's household as a companion and role model for Edward of Caernarfon; he would never have done so if Gaveston had not been of noble birth. Gaveston was charismatic, witty and arrogant, athletic and a great jouster and soldier, and although he had the kind of personality which alienated many people, Edward of Caernarfon became infatuated. By early 1307, Edward I was already concerned about the close, intense, and probably sexual relationship which had developed between the two young men, and what happened at Lanercost Priory brought the matter to crisis point.

Edward of Caernarfon had inherited the county of Ponthieu in northern France from his mother Leonor of Castile on her death in November 1290. Leonor, herself Spanish, had a French mother, Jeanne of Ponthieu, who married the widowed King Fernando III of Castile and Leon in 1237, and was countess of Ponthieu in her own right. Leonor was the second of Jeanne and Fernando's five children, and the only one who outlived her mother; she therefore inherited Ponthieu on Jeanne's death in 1279, and it passed to her only surviving son, Edward of Caernarfon, on her own death. Ponthieu, a small county around the River Somme which no longer exists on the political map of France, bordered the great duchy of Normandy and was a strategically important area in the Middle Ages. After he married Isabella of France in January 1308, Edward II gave Ponthieu to his wife, which was entirely uncontroversial, but in February 1307 he had had another idea: to give it to his cherished Piers Gaveston. Aware that his father would not look favourably on the notion, Edward sent the Bishop of Coventry and Lichfield to put his request to his father on his behalf, at Lanercost Priory.

Edward I reacted with utter fury. Not only did he utterly reject the proposal, he launched a vicious physical attack on his son, supposedly tearing out handfuls of his hair and kicking him to the ground. According to one chronicler, who possibly exaggerated the story, the king even insulted the memory of his beloved late wife Leonor of Castile by calling his son a wretched bastard, or a son of a whore. Edward of Caernarfon was made to swear that he would never give any lands to Gaveston, an oath he broke mere months later after he became king and gave Gaveston the earldom of Cornwall, and the old king decided to banish Gaveston from England to keep him away from his son. This was not so much a punishment of Gaveston himself, but of Edward of Caernarfon. Edward I gave Gaveston a few weeks to set his affairs in order before he left the country and promised him a generous income while he was away, until the king saw fit to recall him. Gaveston went to Edward of Caernarfon's county of Ponthieu rather than his native Béarn and spent a very comfortable few months there, lavished with gifts and money by the infatuated Prince of Wales. And this was not Edward of Caernarfon's first row with his father: in the summer of 1305 the king banished him from court for a while after the young Prince of Wales supposedly shouted foul words at a bishop. The king dissolved his son's household and confiscated his seal.

A chronicle was written (in Latin) by monks of Lanercost Priory which covers all of Edward I and Edward II's reigns and the first few years of Edward III's, and is an extremely valuable source for events in the north of England and in Scotland from the 1270s until the 1340s. A particularly vivid section in the *Chronicle of Lanercost* describes a violent and terrifying thunderstorm in the north of England during the night of 11/12 July 1293 when Edward of Caernarfon was 9, and gives a wonderful insight into the mindset of the era and how they explained natural phenomena:

> We beheld in the east a huge cloud blacker than coal, in the midst whereof we saw the lashes of an immense eye darting fierce lightning into the west, whence I understood that Satan's darts would come from over the sea ... demons were heard yelling in the air.

Edward II's nemesis Robert Bruce, king of Scotland, stayed at Lanercost Priory for a few days with a large army in August 1311, and the indignant and surely biased English chronicler of Lanercost later claimed that the priory suffered 'innumerable evils', a statement which seems certain to be grossly exaggerated. King Robert was surely aware that while Edward I had stayed at Lanercost Priory in early 1307, he had ordered the execution of two of Robert's brothers; Alexander and Thomas Bruce were dragged by horses all the way from Lanercost to Carlisle and were subjected to hanging, drawing and quartering there. Another Bruce brother, Neil or Nigel, had been executed in Berwick-upon-Tweed in September 1306.

Lanercost Priory, founded around 1169 as a house of Augustinian canons, is just south of Hadrian's Wall (a World Heritage Site) and 12 miles from Carlisle, in the far north-west corner of England a few miles from the Scottish border. It lies 40 miles from Caerlaverock Castle, detailed above, and 45 miles west of Newcastle-upon-Tyne. Although it was dissolved in 1538, much of the priory still survives, and is hugely impressive. It is looked after today by English Heritage, and is open to visitors at weekends during winter and every day in summer.

Chapter Two

The First Decade, 1307–1317

Knaresborough Castle, Yorkshire: Possession of Edward's Beloved Gaveston

When Edward II heard in London on 11 July 1307 that his father had died four days earlier, over 300 miles away near Carlisle, almost certainly his first act as king was to recall Piers Gaveston from his exile in Ponthieu. Edward thus set out his main priority and overwhelming concern right from the start of his reign: devotion to Gaveston. Just before he died, Edward I had ordered his son never to allow Gaveston back to England, realising correctly that his son's infatuation with, and favouritism towards, the Béarnais knight was likely to cause huge problems between his son and the English nobility, but Edward II took not an iota of notice.

On 6 August 1307, less than a month into his reign, Edward made Piers Gaveston earl of Cornwall, probably even before Gaveston had returned to court from exile in Ponthieu and been reunited with the new king. The earldom of Cornwall belonged to Edward II personally: the last earl of Cornwall, Edmund, a nephew of Henry III (r. 1216–72), died in 1300, and as he had no children, siblings or nephews and nieces, the earldom passed to his first cousin, Edward I, as his nearest male relative, and then to Edward II on his father's death. Part of the territories of the earldom included the towns of Knaresborough and Boroughbridge in Yorkshire. Knaresborough Castle dates back to around 1100, and was the refuge for the four knights who murdered Thomas Becket, archbishop of Canterbury, in Canterbury Cathedral on 29 December 1170, supposedly on the orders of Edward II's great-great-grandfather Henry II (r. 1154–89). Hugh de Morville, one of the killers, owned Knaresborough, and the other three who fled there with him were William de Tracy, Reginald Fitzurse and

Richard le Breton. The four stayed in Knaresborough for about a year, during which time they were excommunicated by Pope Alexander III, then all set off on a penitential pilgrimage to the Holy Land from which they did not return. The castle passed to Henry II's son and Edward II's great-grandfather King John in 1205, and he spent a lot of money improving it, as did his grandson Edward I at the start of the 1300s. Edward II himself had the great keep built in 1312.

Edward II stayed at Knaresborough from 9 to 12 September 1307 with Gaveston, who had then been earl of Cornwall for just a month and entertained the king and his large retinue at his own expense, and was also there in November 1309. Edward was at Knaresborough again between 11 and 14 May 1312, after he had left Gaveston at Scarborough Castle on the 9th; the siege of Gaveston inside Scarborough began on the same day (see 'Scarborough Castle' below). After Gaveston's execution at Blacklow Hill in Warwickshire on 19 June 1312, Knaresborough Castle reverted to Edward and he kept it in his own hands for the rest of his reign, and stayed there for the last time from 26 February to 17 March 1323.

After Piers Gaveston's death, Edward II was without a male 'favourite' for some years, but reliance on and infatuation with men was an important part of his emotional make-up, and sometime in 1315 he began some kind of association – perhaps sexual, perhaps not – with Sir Roger Damory, a knight of Oxfordshire. Damory was Edward II's powerful 'favourite' between 1315 and 1318, and married the king's widowed niece Elizabeth de Burgh, née de Clare, in 1317. Knaresborough Castle was seized by Edward's cousin and enemy Thomas, earl of Lancaster, in early October 1317, and was not restored to the king until the following January. Almost certainly, this represents an attack by the earl of Lancaster on Sir Roger Damory, the then constable of Knaresborough Castle. The earl of Lancaster loathed Damory, and even accused him of trying to kill him.

Knaresborough Castle later passed to Edward II's daughter-in-law (whom he never met), Philippa of Hainault (c. 1314–69), queen of England, who married his son Edward III in early 1328. Philippa's third son, John of Gaunt (1340–99), duke of Lancaster and one of the richest men in England in the fourteenth century, acquired Knaresborough in 1372, three years after Queen Philippa's death. When John's son and heir became King Henry IV in 1399, the castle returned to the control of the kings of England. It was partially demolished in 1648 after the garrison supported the royalist cause during the Civil War.

Knaresborough Castle is now in ruins, and stands in a public park in the middle of the town. There is no entrance charge to the park which is open to the public at all times, but going inside the King's Tower incurs a small charge, and it is only open from Easter to September. The King's Tower as it exists today was built by Edward II between 1307 and 1312, and a small 'porch' attached to it is believed to have been a waiting room for those who had been summoned to the main chamber on the first floor. The ground dramatically falls away on one side of the castle, and visitors can make their way down steep, stepped paths to the River Nidd; here one can go boating and look up at the castle. From the castle grounds, the town, its railway viaduct and the river make an attractive scene. Knaresborough is a small town 4 miles from Harrogate and 20 miles from Leeds, and can easily be reached by public transport or road from either place.

Berkhamsted Castle, Hertfordshire: Gaveston Weds Edward's Niece

Berkhamsted Castle belonged to Edward II's stepmother Queen Marguerite, and is where his dearest friend and probable lover Piers Gaveston, the new earl of Cornwall, married Edward's niece, Margaret de Clare, in November 1307. Marguerite of France was born in 1278 or 1279, and was the younger half-sister of King Philip IV (b. 1268, r. 1285–1314). Philip IV went to war against Edward I – his father's first cousin – in 1294, and to make peace some years later, arranged his half-sister's marriage to the English king. His toddler daughter Isabella's future marriage to Edward of Caernarfon was arranged at the same time and for the same reason. Marguerite, aged 20, duly married the 60-year-old Edward I in Canterbury on 8 September 1299. They had two sons, Edward of Caernarfon's much younger half-brothers Thomas of Brotherton and Edmund of Woodstock, born in June 1300 and August 1301, and a daughter, Eleanor, born in May 1306 who died young, before Edward I died at the age of 68 on 7 July 1307. Marguerite became a widow when she was still only in her 20s, and lived until February 1318. She and her stepson Edward, only five years her junior, appear to have been on good terms during his father's lifetime, but that was to end when Edward became king and Marguerite showed her hostility to Piers Gaveston. For the remaining ten years of her life, Edward almost entirely ignored Marguerite. Edward II was the first king of England since before the Norman Conquest of 1066 to have a stepmother, and the next would be his great-great-grandson Henry V (b. 1386, r. 1413–22), whose relationship with his own stepmother Juana of Navarre (c. 1370–1437) became so bad in 1419 that Henry imprisoned her on charges of trying to poison him by witchcraft.

In addition to making Gaveston earl of Cornwall on 6 August 1307, Edward wished to bring him into the royal family by marriage. None of Edward's surviving sisters were available: Mary was a nun, Margaret was married to the duke of Brabant and Elizabeth to the earl of Hereford, and his half-sister Eleanor, Queen Marguerite's daughter, was only 18 months old. Edward therefore had to turn to his nieces, and the oldest one still unmarried was 13-year-old Margaret de Clare, second daughter of Edward's sister Joan of Acre, countess of Gloucester (1272 – April 1307). Piers Gaveston was much older than his new wife; she was probably born in the spring or summer of 1294, and he was born in the early 1280s, perhaps even in the 1270s. And so a barely pubescent girl married a much older man who was involved in an intense, obsessive and almost certainly sexual relationship with her own uncle, and who over the next few months and years made himself the most hated man in England.

Edward II spent a fortune on food, drink and minstrels to entertain the wedding guests at Berkhamsted on 1 November 1307, and they must have had quite a wild time as the king had to pay compensation to a local resident for damage done to his property during the wedding celebrations. Edward provided the generous amount of £7 – well over a year's income for most of his subjects – in penny coins to be thrown over the heads of the newlyweds. This was a popular contemporary custom intended to bring the couple good luck, and the coins were later collected and distributed to the poor as alms. Edward also bought his niece a fine and costly palfrey horse, perhaps as a kind of bribe to persuade her to marry Gaveston, though Margaret had little choice. Given her youth at the time of her wedding, she and Gaveston most likely did not begin to live together as husband and wife, and their only child, or at least their only surviving child, was born in January 1312.

Gaveston's supercilious arrogance, and the infatuated king's excessive favouritism towards him, was already beginning to push many of the English barons into opposition, and their antagonism was shared by the dowager Queen Marguerite, the step-grandmother of Margaret Gaveston.

An anonymous newsletter circulated in England in May 1308 stated that Queen Marguerite and her half-brother Philip IV of France had given £40,000 to aid the baronial opposition to Piers Gaveston. This is an impossibly large sum of money and must be a clerical error; even £4,000 would have been Marguerite's entire income for a year. Still, it seems beyond doubt that Marguerite had offered support to her stepson's enemies.

Marguerite of France lived quietly for the remaining decade of her life, mostly at her castle of Marlborough in Wiltshire, and there is little evidence that Edward II kept in touch with her; evidently he refused to forgive her for her opposition to Gaveston in 1308. She died at Marlborough on 14 February 1318 in her late thirties or early forties, leaving her sons Thomas and Edmund, then teenagers. Edward attended her funeral at the Greyfriars church in London that March. Marguerite's lands and castles, including Berkhamsted, passed to the lady who was both her niece and her stepson's wife: Isabella of France, queen of England. In 1337, Isabella and Edward II's son, Edward III, gave it to his eldest son Edward of Woodstock (1330–76), later Prince of Wales, as part of the new duchy of Cornwall he had bestowed on the boy. Edward of Woodstock married Joan of Kent in 1361, and they spent their honeymoon at Berkhamsted Castle and their first Christmas there.

Berkhamsted Castle was abandoned as a residence at the end of the fifteenth century and within fifty years was ruinous, and was subsequently plundered for stone by local builders. The construction of a railway line in 1838 destroyed the barbican, or outer gate. There are, however, still extensive walls, ditches and earthworks, now looked after by English Heritage. The castle dates back to about 1070 and was built by William the Conqueror's brother Robert, count of Mortain (d. 1090). Edward II's great-great-grandfather Henry II (b. 1133, r. 1154–89) gave Berkhamsted to Thomas Becket in 1155, the archbishop of Canterbury, whom he later had murdered in Canterbury Cathedral.

At the end of the reign of Henry II's youngest son King John, Edward II's great-grandfather, the future King Louis VIII of France, invaded England at the behest of many of John's dissatisfied barons. Louis besieged Berkhamsted Castle for two weeks before he was defeated at the battle of Lincoln in 1217 and retreated to France. Edward II's great-uncle Richard, earl of Cornwall (1209–72), younger son of King John and brother of Henry III, was given Berkhamsted in 1225 and rebuilt it in palatial style; his younger son and eventual heir Edmund, earl of Cornwall, was born there in late 1249.

The castle is open most days of the year and lies next to Berkhamsted railway station. It is just 8 miles from Edward II's favourite residence of Kings Langley and 30 miles from London.

Wallingford Castle, Oxfordshire (formerly in Berkshire): Gaveston's Great Jousting Tournament

Wallingford Castle passed to Piers Gaveston in 1307 as part of the earldom of Cornwall, and had previously belonged to Henry III's brother Richard of Cornwall (1209–72) and Richard's son and heir Edmund (1249–1300). After Gaveston's death in June 1312, Edward did not give the earldom of Cornwall to anyone else. It did eventually pass to his own second son John of Eltham (b. August 1316), but only in October 1328 after Edward II's deposition and death, early in the reign of his elder son Edward III. In the meantime, Edward II had given Wallingford Castle to his queen Isabella of France, in 1317, and it was here, over Christmas 1326, that Edward II's fate was debated and decided. Isabella had invaded her husband's kingdom in late September 1326 intending to bring down his last, loathed, and most powerful male favourite, Hugh Despenser the Younger. She and her advisers decided at Wallingford that Edward II must be made to abdicate his throne to his elder son, Edward of Windsor, who became Edward III in January 1327 (and who had grown up partly at Wallingford Castle). Edward III made his first son Edward of Woodstock duke of Cornwall in 1337, and Wallingford Castle belonged to him until his death in June 1376. Edward of Woodstock's widow Joan of Kent, dowager princess of Wales and a niece of Edward II, died at Wallingford in August 1385.

Piers Gaveston, earl of Cornwall, married Edward II's niece Margaret de Clare at Berkhamsted Castle on 1 November 1307, and a month later held a great jousting tournament at Wallingford Castle to celebrate becoming a member of the English royal family. The king himself did not attend, staying at his Hertfordshire manor of Langley, but the earls of Hereford, Surrey and Arundel participated in the joust. Gaveston and his team of young knights defeated the three earls, and destroyed their dignity by knocking them off their horses into the mud.

Indignant chroniclers claimed that Gaveston 'most vilely trod under foot' the opposition, and accused him of cheating by fielding 200 knights instead of the agreed sixty. Gaveston was a champion jouster, and according to one chronicler held a tournament at Faversham in Kent in February 1308 to celebrate Edward II's recent marriage to Isabella of France (the pair wed in France in January 1308). Edward II himself stayed at Wallingford from 22 to 26 April 1318 and from 29 April to 4 May 1321. Wallingford Castle featured again in Edward's story in early 1323. The king imprisoned some of the barons who had taken part in a rebellion against him in 1321/22 at Wallingford Castle. Sir Hugh Audley and Maurice, Lord Berkeley almost escaped in early 1323 when they overcame their guards and took over the castle. One chronicler says that only the quick thinking of a boy in the gatehouse, who realised that something was amiss and raised the hue and cry, prevented their escape, while another chronicler claims that Lord Berkeley's wife Isabella captured Wallingford Castle and held it for a fortnight.

The town of Wallingford stands on the River Thames about 13 miles from Oxford and was an important crossing-point of the river during the Middle Ages. The castle was built just after the Norman Conquest of 1066, and during the Anarchy of the 1130s and 1140s, when both King Stephen and his first cousin the Empress Maud claimed the English throne, it was in the hands of Maud's staunch supporter Brian FitzCount. King Stephen therefore besieged Wallingford in 1139, 1145/46 and 1152/53. He also besieged his cousin Maud at Oxford Castle in 1141. Her near-miraculous escape, when she and a group of supporters dressed themselves in white and abseiled down the castle walls during the night and made their way through Stephen's besieging army in the deep snow to the safety of nearby Wallingford, is the stuff of legend. Maud's grandson King John, Edward II's great-grandfather, was given Wallingford by his older brother Richard Lionheart after he came to the throne in 1189; in 1191 John held out at the castle for a while during a brief revolt against his brother. In 1231, Wallingford passed to John's younger son Richard, earl of Cornwall, who renovated it and built a new hall.

After about 1518, during Henry VIII's reign, Wallingford appears to have fallen out of use as a residence and was stripped and used for building materials during the reign of Queen Mary (r. 1553–58). There was still enough of it left in 1646, however, for royalist forces to hold and defend for several months against the parliamentarian general,

Sir Thomas Fairfax. In common with many English castles, after the Civil War it was 'slighted', or mostly destroyed. Some walls still exist, as well as the ditch and massive earthworks, of the once great castle where a royal favourite once sent some of the great earls of the realm sprawling into the mud during a jousting tournament. The site belongs to South Oxfordshire District Council and is open to the public every day of the year, and information about the castle and its history can be found in the Wallingford Museum in the town, nearby.

Dover Castle, Kent: Edward's Bride Arrives in England

Edward II's marriage to Isabella of France, which took place in January 1308, had been arranged as far back as 1299 and was intended to cement the recent peace settlement between their warring fathers Edward I and Philip IV. Edward of Caernarfon was 15 years old in 1299; Isabella, probably born in late 1295, was not yet 4. She was the third but only surviving daughter of Philip IV of France and Jeanne I, queen-regnant of Navarre in Spain (r. 1274–1305), and all three of her older brothers, Louis X, Philip V and Charles IV, reigned as kings of France and Navarre. Betrothed to Edward of Caernarfon when she was only a toddler, Isabella cannot have remembered a time when she did not know that it was her destiny to become Edward's queen, and as the daughter of a king and a queen-regnant and royal to her very fingertips, Isabella must have been delighted at the prospect.

The couple, though engaged since 1299, did not meet in person until the day of their wedding, Thursday, 25 January 1308. Edward II spent Christmas 1307, the first of his reign, at Westminster, and on 26 December scandalously made Piers Gaveston the 'keeper of the realm' in his absence while he travelled to France to marry Isabella. The 23-year-old king – with Piers Gaveston in his company – stayed at Dover Castle from 13 to 22 January 1308, then sailed from Dover to Wissant leaving Gaveston behind in Dover as regent of England. Edward arrived several days late for his wedding, almost certainly because of adverse weather conditions in the English Channel; it was, after all, the depths of winter, and there is no reason at all to suppose that he intended any insult to the French or to his fiancée, as some modern writers have speculated. He and his retinue rode to Boulogne, where on 25 January he married Isabella in a splendid ceremony attended by her father the king of France, her eldest brother the king of Navarre and her other two brothers, and a whole host of English, French and European royalty and nobility.

Edward II and Isabella of France returned to Dover in the middle of the afternoon on Wednesday, 7 February 1308. This was the first time the 12-year-old new queen of England set foot in the land which would be her home for the remaining half a century of her life. (Sir William Wallace, with whom the film *Braveheart* depicts Isabella having an affair that results in her son, had been executed on 23 August 1305, so she cannot possibly have met him.) Edward II had arranged a welcome party to wait at Dover for his and Isabella's arrival, including his sisters Elizabeth, countess of Hereford, and Mary, a nun of Amesbury in Wiltshire, and the earl of Lancaster's younger brother Henry of Lancaster, who was both his first cousin and Isabella's uncle. Also waiting at Dover, and a person perhaps rather less to Isabella's liking, was Piers Gaveston. Edward made a big fuss of Piers when he arrived at Dover, kissing and hugging him, though whether Isabella saw this is not clear, as she and Edward arrived on shore in separate barges. Although it is likely that Edward and Gaveston were lovers, Edward's behaviour on this occasion does not automatically prove it, as the early fourteenth century was an era when men were far more tactile with one another than is the case nowadays, and easily threw around declarations of love for each other. To Edward's contemporaries, the problem was not so much that Edward hugged and kissed Piers Gaveston in public, but that he discourteously ignored the other barons present to do so, and thus showed Gaveston excessive favouritism. What, if anything, Isabella of France already knew about Gaveston and her husband's relationship with him cannot be known, nor how they got along over the coming months and years, but the frequent assumption that she hated him and considered him her rival for her husband's affections is just that, an assumption, not backed up by any real evidence. The king and queen left Dover on 10 February 1308 and travelled through Kent to the Tower of London, where they stayed for several nights before their joint coronation at Westminster Abbey on 25 February. If Isabella had been unaware of the prominent position Piers Gaveston held in her husband's life, their coronation would soon have made it all too apparent; Gaveston played an important role in the coronation ceremony itself, and organised the banquet afterwards.

Dover Castle towers over the white cliffs of the south of England, and to this day makes a remarkably impressive sight for visitors arriving from Calais by ferry. It was the first glimpse of England Isabella had, and the first place in England where she slept. Dover Castle is called 'the key to England', and is one of the largest castles in Britain. Almost certainly the site was already fortified in Roman times, and Edward II's great-great-grandfather Henry II built the castle as it stands today. In 1265, Edward I besieged his own aunt Eleanor (c. 1215–75), King Henry's sister, and wife of the rebel earl of Leicester, Simon de Montfort (c. 1208–65), at Dover Castle. Edward II did not spend much time at Dover, but visited for a few days in August 1312 a few weeks after Piers Gaveston's death, when he put his royal castles on a war footing against the barons who had killed Gaveston. While at Dover Castle in the summer of 1312, he paid an Italian man, John of Lombardy, £1 for 'making his minstrelsy with snakes before the king'.

Edward II was also at Dover Castle in late August and early September 1325 when he made a fateful decision which was to bring about his downfall and forced deposition little more than a year later. As duke of Aquitaine and count of Ponthieu, Edward owed homage to the king of France as his overlord for the French territories, and every time a new king of France succeeded to the throne, he had to travel to France to participate in the ceremony of homage. In 1323/24, Edward II was so reluctant to leave England in order to swear homage to Charles IV (the third and last of Queen Isabella's brothers) that he offered endless excuses and kept delaying, until finally an exasperated Charles invaded the duchy of Aquitaine. In the summer of 1324, England and France went to war in a little-known conflict called the War of Saint-Sardos. Edward sent Isabella, his wife and Charles's sister, to France in March 1325 to arrange a peace settlement, which she achieved, but the vexed question of homage remained. Either Edward travelled to France to perform the ceremony, or he and his successors would lose their French lands permanently; but Edward's incompetence and support for Hugh Despenser the Younger's despotism meant that his kingdom seethed with unrest and he did not want rebellion to break out in his absence. He therefore decided, after changing his mind on an almost daily basis for weeks on end, to send his son Edward of Windsor in his place. The boy, born on 13 November 1312 and not yet 13 years old, sailed to France from Dover on 12 September 1325. Edward II never saw his son again; Isabella of France refused to allow the boy to return to England, and used her son as a weapon to try to force Edward to send Hugh Despenser the Younger, a man the queen loathed and feared, away. Edward would not do so, and Isabella and their son ultimately returned to England at the head of an invasion force in September 1326. This was the beginning of the end for Edward II.

Dover's history dates back thousands of years, and the castle remained an important site even into the twentieth century; the tunnels under the castle, dug in Napoleonic times, were used as the command centre for naval operations in the Channel, and in 1941 an underground hospital was opened to treat injured troops. A late twelfth-century royal palace has been recreated in the Great Tower of Dover Castle, as Edward II's great-great-grandfather Henry II would have known it, and on some days of the year the palace is vividly brought to life by actors. Dover Castle is now managed by English Heritage, and is open every day of the year between spring and autumn, though only at weekends in winter. The town of Dover is 75 miles from central London, and 37 miles from Leeds Castle, detailed elsewhere in this volume.

Stamford, Lincolnshire: Edward Holds Parliament

Edward II held a short parliament in the town of Stamford early in his reign; he arrived there on 26 or 27 July 1309 and stayed until 5 August. Edward's baronial enemies had forced Piers Gaveston into exile from England in June 1308, and he was stripped of his earldom of Cornwall. The king turned disaster into triumph by appointing Gaveston as his lord lieutenant of Ireland, and spent a year manipulating his barons until they consented to Gaveston's return. He returned in late June 1309, almost exactly a year to the day after his departure, and at the Stamford parliament Edward II restored him to his earldom of Cornwall, and to him and his wife Margaret de Clare's (the king's niece) many lands in England. Edward visited Stamford again from 22 to 24 October 1315; he had spent a cheery holiday from mid-September to mid-October swimming and rowing in the Fens near Cambridge, and was on his way to his Nottinghamshire hunting-lodge of Clipstone with Queen Isabella. The royal couple must have conceived their second son John of Eltham, later earl of Cornwall, born on 15 August 1316, around this time; perhaps when they were in Stamford.

One of Edward II's many nieces was Joan of Kent, the daughter and ultimate heir of his much younger half-brother Edmund of Woodstock, earl of Kent (1301–30). Joan was born either in September 1326 or in' September 1327 (according to the evidence of her brother John's Inquisition Post Mortem in December 1352), and hence never knew her uncle Edward, who was supposedly murdered at Berkeley Castle in September 1327, perhaps the month of her birth. Her father, Edmund, earl of Kent, was executed in March 1330 after becoming convinced that his half-brother Edward II – who by then had supposedly been dead for two-and-a-half years – was still alive, and with a large group of followers plotted to free Edward from captivity and perhaps restore him to his lost throne. Joan of Kent later became countess of Kent in her own right after the deaths of her two brothers, and married her third husband, Edward III's eldest son and heir, Edward of Woodstock, Prince of Wales, in 1361. Edward II's niece thus married his grandson.

Joan of Kent and Edward of Woodstock were the parents of Richard II, who was born in Bordeaux in southern France in January 1367 when his mother was about 40, and who succeeded his grandfather Edward III to the throne in June 1377. Richard II was both Edward II's great-grandson and his great-nephew.

Joan of Kent's first husband, Sir Thomas Holland, was buried at the church of the Franciscans, also sometimes called the Greyfriars, in Stamford, Lincolnshire, when he died at the end of 1360, and in her will of 1385 Joan asked to be buried with him rather than with her far more prestigious third husband, the Prince of Wales, at Canterbury Cathedral. Her son Richard II, whether he was happy about her request or not, duly had her interred there. Two of the grandsons of Edward II's last and most powerful favourite Hugh Despenser the Younger were also buried at the Greyfriars Church in Stamford in 1374 and 1381.

In the twenty-first century, Stamford is a picturesque town of about 22,000 inhabitants which stands on the River Welland, 92 miles north of London, 45 miles south-east of Nottingham and 75 miles east of Birmingham. It is in the county of Lincolnshire, very close to the Cambridgeshire border. There are five medieval churches and a large number of half-timbered and stone houses dating from the seventeenth century and earlier; Edward II would recognise much of All Saints' Church and St Mary's, and probably St John the Baptist's. The Greyfriars Church, where his niece Joan of Kent and Hugh Despenser the Younger's grandsons were buried in the 1370s and 1380s, no longer exists, with the exception of its gatehouse which dates to the second quarter of the fourteenth century, just after Edward's reign. Standing halfway between York and London, the town of Stamford became prosperous in the seventeenth and eighteenth centuries as a staging post for the wool trade, and has sometimes been used in the late twentieth and twenty-first centuries as a location for TV programmes and films, notably *Pride and Prejudice* and *The Da Vinci Code*. Burghley House, one of England's finest Elizabethan houses and built by Elizabeth I's Lord High Treasurer Sir William Cecil (with a park laid out by Capability Brown in the eighteenth century), is just outside Stamford, over the border in Cambridgeshire.

Beaulieu Abbey, Hampshire: Funeral of Edward's Half-Sister

Edward II was the youngest of his mother Leonor of Castile's fourteen or more children. He lost his mother in November 1290 when he was 6, and his father Edward I remained a widower for nine years. On 8 September 1299, 60-year-old Edward married his second wife, 20-year-old Marguerite of France. Marguerite became pregnant immediately and gave birth to her first child Thomas of Brotherton, later earl of Norfolk, on 1 June 1300, one week short of nine months after her wedding. Her second son, Edmund of Woodstock, later earl of Kent (and King Richard II's grandfather), followed on 5 August 1301. Edward and Marguerite's third and youngest child was born in May 1306, a few weeks before Edward's sixty-seventh birthday, and was named Eleanor in honour of his first wife Leonor 'or Eleanor' of Castile. When Eleanor was only four days old, her father began negotiations for her to marry Robert, heir to the counties of Burgundy and Artois in France. Sadly, the little girl died shortly before 28 August 1311 at the age of only 5, and her much older half-brother Edward II paid the large sum of £113 'for the expenses and preparations made for the burial of the body of the Lady Eleanor, the king's sister' at Beaulieu Abbey in Hampshire.

Edward II spent most of April 1325 staying at Beaulieu Abbey, and presumably took the time to visit his little half-sister's grave while there. The king himself, as unconventional as ever, went fishing near the abbey with a local fisherman called Jack Bere and seven unnamed others on this occasion. Most medieval kings enjoyed the sport of jousting; Edward never participated, and preferred fishing. A few months previously in June 1324 when visiting Tonbridge Castle in Kent, he borrowed a boat from a local man also to go fishing, apparently on his own.

Beaulieu Abbey was a house belonging to the strict and austere Cistercian order. Although Edward's chamberlain and 'favourite' Hugh Despenser the Younger stayed there with the king in April 1325, Despenser's wife and Edward's beloved niece Eleanor, née de Clare, were not allowed to. Women could not spend the night at Cistercian houses, but Eleanor must have stayed somewhere nearby, as there is a record of Edward giving her a gift of 100 marks or £66 while he was at Beaulieu, apparently on hearing the news of her latest pregnancy. Eleanor was the older sister of Margaret de Clare, who had married Piers Gaveston in 1307. She herself married Hugh Despenser the Younger on 26 May 1306 at Westminster, in the presence of her grandfather Edward I and her uncle Edward of Caernarfon, a little over a year before the old king died.

Beaulieu Abbey was founded at the beginning of the 1200s by Edward II's great-grandfather King John, and the name means 'beautiful place' in French and is pronounced 'bewley' in modern English. John's son Richard of Cornwall (1209–72), Edward's great-uncle, buried his first wife Isabella, a daughter of William Marshal, earl of Pembroke, at Beaulieu in 1240. Six years later, Richard founded a daughter house of Beaulieu, Hailes Abbey in Gloucestershire. Also in 1246, Richard and his brother Henry III and Henry's queen Eleanor of Provence (c. 1223–91) (Edward II's grandparents) were present when Beaulieu was finally completed and consecrated; the future King Edward I also attended, and the date of consecration was his seventh birthday, 17 June 1246. Beaulieu Abbey was an important royal foundation and was declared as an 'exempt abbey' by Pope Innocent III (1198–1216), meaning that the abbot answered to the pope alone and not to the local bishop. Edward II's burial of his little half-sister Eleanor there in 1311 was therefore a mark of great honour, and a sign of his affection for her (despite his anger with her mother Queen Marguerite).

Beaulieu Abbey was closed down in 1538 during the Dissolution, and the abbey church, cloisters and chapter-house were demolished. The refectory and two gatehouses were, however, left standing, and can be seen today. Beaulieu is located in the New Forest, 10 miles from Southampton, 26 from Salisbury and 90 from London. There is a visitor attraction called

'Beaulieu' with its own website, and tickets can be purchased in advance for the abbey and other locations nearby including the National Motor Museum and the thirteenth-century Beaulieu Palace House.

Scarborough Castle, Yorkshire: Gaveston is Besieged

After Piers Gaveston, earl of Cornwall, returned to England from his second exile in Ireland in late June 1309, he demonstrated that neither he nor Edward II had learned anything at all from the experience, and they carried on exactly as they had before; with the king showing Gaveston excessive favouritism and showering him with lands, appointments, gifts and favours. Gaveston, who had a sharp tongue and did not care whom he offended, made matters even worse by giving several of the powerful English earls insulting nicknames. In March 1310, a group of concerned earls, barons and bishops formed themselves into a group called the Lords Ordainer, and appointed themselves to reform Edward II's household and government. Their reforms were finally presented to the king in September 1311, and to his horror they limited his executive powers considerably. The twentieth of the forty-one Ordinances, as they were called, banished Piers Gaveston forever from all of Edward II's territories, i.e. England, Wales, Ireland, Ponthieu in northern France, and even Gaveston's native Gascony in southern France. This closed the loophole whereby Edward had previously sent Gaveston to Ireland to act as his lord lieutenant, and was the Ordinance which caused the king the most grief. He promised to abide by all the others if the barons would only let Piers Gaveston stay with him, and alternated between hurling angry threats at them and trying to bribe them with favours and gifts, but they remained firm. Gaveston, once more stripped of his earldom of Cornwall and banished from England for the third time, left the country in early November 1311; where he went is not clear, but perhaps to the continental duchy of Brabant whose capital was Brussels, where Edward II's brother-in-law Duke John II and sister Margaret (b. 1275) ruled. Gaveston's 17-year-old pregnant wife Margaret, the king's niece and the earl of Gloucester's sister, remained in England and lived at Wallingford Castle.

Gaveston returned from his supposedly perpetual third exile only two months later in early 1312, perhaps for the birth of his child and heir,

Joan Gaveston, but Edward II took matters out of his hands, restored him to the earldom of Cornwall and declared him 'good and loyal'. King and favourite spent months skulking in the north of England hiding away from the Lords Ordainer, their powerful baronial enemies, in the south. Chief among Gaveston's enemies was Thomas, earl of Lancaster and Leicester, Edward II's first cousin and Queen Isabella's uncle. Thomas came close to capturing Piers Gaveston, and the king himself, at Tynemouth Priory (see below) on 4 May 1312, and the two men had to escape down the coast in a small boat. They sailed to Scarborough, and Edward left Gaveston in the castle while he headed to York via Knaresborough in an unsuccessful attempt to raise support. Edward had visited Scarborough in late February 1312, but had not had the foresight to prepare it for a siege.

The king set off for Knaresborough on 10 May 1312 leaving Gaveston inside Scarborough Castle, and on the same day, the earls of Pembroke and Surrey and lords Clifford and Percy arrived to besiege Piers Gaveston inside the castle. Aymer de Valence, earl of Pembroke, was a first cousin once removed of the king, and John de Warenne, earl of Surrey, Edward's nephew-in-law, and both men were usually loyal allies of the king, but his antics and obstinacy over Gaveston had proved too much for them. Piers Gaveston had to surrender to the magnates after a siege of only nine days on 19 May 1312, as he and the other men inside had little or no food. He probably met the king one last time in York, and it was agreed that Edward's cousin the earl of Pembroke should take Gaveston south to his own castle of Wallingford near Oxford, and that a session of parliament would meet in the south of England to debate and decide his fate.

Scarborough Castle was built in the twelfth and early thirteenth centuries by Edward II's great-great-grandfather Henry II and great-grandfather King John, though it stands on a site which has been inhabited and fortified for at least 3,000 years. The extensive castle ruins stand on a headland with impressive views over the North Sea a mile from Scarborough railway station, under 20 miles from Pickering Castle (see elsewhere in this volume) and 40 miles from York. It is looked after nowadays by English Heritage, and there is also a Roman signal station on the site. The great tower which Edward II and Piers Gaveston would have known, built in the 1160s by Henry II, still dominates the landscape, and there are remains of a hall within the inner bailey built by Henry's son King John in the early 1200s which Edward II would also have known.

Warwick Castle, Warwickshire: Gaveston is Imprisoned and Killed

Edward II and Piers Gaveston kept in touch via letters during Gaveston's journey from York to Gaveston's own castle of Wallingford as a prisoner of the earl of Pembroke, until 10 June, when Gaveston and Pembroke reached the Oxfordshire town of Deddington. Here, Gaveston's chief enemy Guy Beauchamp, earl of Warwick, seized an opportunity for revenge on the royal favourite who had mocked him as 'the Black Hound of Arden'. Aymer de Valence, earl of Pembroke, left Gaveston under guard at the priory of Deddington while he went to spend the night with his French wife Beatrice de Clermont-Nesle a few miles away. The earl of Warwick decided to take advantage. On Saturday, 10 June 1312, Piers Gaveston was awakened by the arrival of the earl and a large crowd of his armed men. The earl's men dragged him outside barefoot, tore his belt of knighthood from him, and made him walk through the streets of Deddington in front of a jeering crowd. He was then put on a mangy horse and taken the 30 miles to Warwick Castle, and cast into a dungeon there, in chains.

The earl of Warwick sent word to his allies the earls of Lancaster, Hereford and Arundel, and the men decided that Piers Gaveston must be put to death. They gave him no trial and no chance to defend himself, and probably could see no alternative to killing him; if they exiled him for the fourth time, Edward II would only recall him yet again, and civil war would break out. On 19 June 1312, the earl of Warwick sent a messenger to his prisoner in the dungeon, and the man told Gaveston, 'Look to yourself, my lord, for today you will die the death.'

The royal favourite was removed from his dungeon, and taken 2 miles along the road towards Kenilworth until they reached Blacklow Hill, which lay on Lancaster's lands (and is just outside the village of Leek Wootton). The earl of Warwick lost his nerve and remained in his castle, while the earl of Lancaster, Edward II's first cousin and by far the richest, most powerful and most royal of the English earls of the era, took responsibility for the bloody act. He ordered Gaveston to be run through with a sword, then as he lay dying on the ground, his head was cut off. The earls returned hastily to Warwick Castle, leaving Gaveston's body on the ground. A group of Dominican friars of Oxford took the body back to their house, embalmed it and sewed the head back on; Gaveston's body would remain at their house until the king finally had him buried two-and-a-half years later at the beginning of 1315. A number of precious items were discovered on the body, and they were returned to Edward II. The king learned of Gaveston's death a week later on 26 June 1312 when he was in York, and made his way south to London. Various chroniclers comment on his terrible rage and grief. During the journey from York to London, evidently in an attempt to take his mind off his bereavement, Edward hired minstrels: Janin the Conjuror, who performed tricks for him in his private chamber at Swineshead Priory in Lincolnshire, a group of acrobats who 'made vaults' before him, and Gracios the Taborer, a kind of drummer.

Warwick Castle, near the River Avon, was originally built by William the Conqueror shortly after 1066, and was much enlarged and rebuilt by its owners throughout the Middle Ages. From 1088 onwards it belonged to the earls of Warwick, at first the Beaumont family and, from 1267 onwards, the Beauchamps, until 1449 when Anne Beauchamp and her husband Richard Neville, the 'Kingmaker', inherited it. Warwick Castle is only about 5 miles from Kenilworth Castle, and is situated conveniently close to Birmingham International Airport and 20 miles from central Birmingham. Ample parking is provided close to the castle, and it stands about a mile from Warwick railway station from where there is a direct connection to London Marylebone. A Warwick Castle Express coach leaves London three times a week from April to November. Tickets to visit the castle can be purchased in advance online, and a Warwick Castle annual pass allows unlimited entry for a year. Overnight accommodation at the castle is available in woodland lodges and medieval 'glamping' within the Knight's Village, or more luxuriously in the Tower Suites in the fourteenth-century Caesar's Tower. Numerous attractions are provided at the castle, including a tour of the dungeon where Piers Gaveston was once imprisoned, a Horrible Histories maze, and 64 acres of landscaped gardens.

Windsor Castle, Berkshire: Birth of Edward's Son and Heir

Edward II's son and successor Edward III was born at Windsor Castle on Monday, 13 November 1312, and until his accession to the throne in January 1327 was often known as Edward of Windsor. His father bestowed the earldom of Chester on him when he was only a few days old. Assuming a full-term pregnancy of thirty-eight weeks from the date of conception, Edward III must have been conceived on, or not long after, 21 February 1312 when his parents were in York, and was probably conceived days after the expensive festivities paid for by Edward II to celebrate the birth of his great-niece Joan Gaveston, and the 'purification' (a ceremony held forty days after childbirth) of his niece Margaret Gaveston, née de Clare, on 20 February. Easter Sunday fell on 26 March in 1312, so Edward II and Queen Isabella conceived their son during Lent, when intercourse was officially forbidden by the Church.

Piers Gaveston, earl of Cornwall, was executed in Warwickshire on 19 June 1312 when Queen Isabella was four months pregnant, and Edward II left her behind in Yorkshire to keep her out of the way of danger when he travelled south to London at the end of June. Gaveston's killers, the earls of Lancaster, Warwick, Hereford and Arundel, raised armies and brought them to Hertfordshire, not far from London, and for a while in the summer of 1312, it seemed as though war would break out in England between the king and some of his powerful barons. Thankfully, however, it did not. Edward's nephew, the young earl of Gloucester, was one of the men who mediated between the two sides and averted war, as were several others sent by Queen Isabella's father Philip IV of France, including Philip's own half-brother Louis, count of Evreux. Judging that it was now safe enough for his wife to come south, King Edward sent for Queen Isabella in early September, and the royal couple retired to Windsor Castle on 17 September 1312, in preparation for the birth. While they were there, Edward paid a Welsh minstrel to perform for them, and gave Isabella permission to make her will. As a married woman she needed his consent to do so, and making a will while expecting was a common thing for women to do in the fourteenth century; pregnancy and childbirth carried immense risks. Isabella's uncle Louis, count of Evreux, stayed with the royal couple at Windsor for a few weeks, and so did Louis's sister Marguerite, dowager queen of England, Edward I's widow and Edward II's stepmother. This was one of the very few occasions, perhaps the only occasion, that Marguerite and Edward II spent any time together after she showed her hostility to Piers Gaveston in 1308.

Edward II was 28 when his son and heir was born, and Queen Isabella was either 17, or very shortly to turn 17. Two contemporary writers, the royal clerk who wrote the *Vita Edwardi Secundi* (Life of Edward II) and the St Albans chronicler, both state that the king's joy at his son's birth considerably lessened the terrible grief he felt over Piers Gaveston's death five months before. The king must also have been delighted that he had secured the succession to his throne, and little Edward of Windsor's birth displaced his 12-year-old uncle Thomas of Brotherton, Queen Marguerite's son and the elder of Edward II's two half-brothers, as the king's heir. Had anything happened to Edward II between his accession in July 1307 and the birth of his son in November 1312, England would have had its first King Thomas. Edward of Windsor was Edward II's first legitimate child, but not his eldest child: he had fathered an illegitimate son named Adam sometime between 1305 and 1310.

The writer of the *Vita Edwardi Secundi* expressed a wish that little Edward of Windsor would grow up to emulate the wisdom of his grandfather Edward I, the longevity of his great-grandfather Henry III (who reigned for fifty-six years and lived to be 65) and the valour of King Richard Lionheart (r. 1189–99), and would 'remind us of the physical strength and comeliness of his father'. Evidently, Edward II's good looks and magnificent physique were the only positive attributes the author could think of to describe him. Edward's subjects, especially in London, celebrated the news of the birth of their future ruler with joy, dancing in the streets and drinking huge amounts of free wine for an entire week, and Tuesday, 14 November 1312 was proclaimed as a public holiday, at least in London. The little boy was baptised at Windsor Castle when he was 3 days old, and had seven godfathers, one of them the Bishop of Worcester and future archbishop of Canterbury, Walter Reynolds (d. 1327). Another was the royalist baron Hugh Despenser the Elder, who was 51 years old in 1312 and whom Edward II made earl of Winchester ten years later. Shortly before he turned 14, in October 1326, Edward of Windsor would see this godfather hanged in Bristol.

Windsor Castle is the oldest and largest occupied castle in the world, and was first built, like so many other castles in Britain, by William the Conqueror and intended as one of a ring of fortifications surrounding London. Edward II's parents, Edward I and Leonor of Castile, spent much time at Windsor; two of Edward II's sisters, Eleanor, countess of Bar (1269–98) and Margaret, Duchess of Brabant (1275–c. 1333) were born at Windsor Castle. Edward I and Queen Leonor's second son Henry was also born at Windsor in 1268, and died at the age of 6 in 1274. Had he lived he would have become King Henry IV of England on his father's death in July 1307, but his own death in October 1274 made his younger brother Alfonso of Bayonne heir to the English throne, and Alfonso held that position until he died in August 1284 when Edward of Caernarfon was four months old.

Edward II did not spend as much time at Windsor as his father Edward I, or his son Edward III, and unlike most of the other medieval English kings, spent little money reinforcing, improving or adding to the castle. He was there in April 1308, during one of the many occasions when he almost led his country to civil war: he refused to banish Piers Gaveston as a large group of his magnates, led by Henry Lacy, earl of Lincoln, were demanding, and retreated inside the safety of Windsor Castle's massive walls. Another royal visit took place in April and May 1317, when Edward attended the weddings of his nieces Margaret Gaveston, née de Clare, and her younger sister Elizabeth de Burgh to his two chief current favourites, Sir Hugh Audley and Sir Roger Damory.

The king was at Windsor again on 11 July 1326, when he dined in the park with his eldest and favourite niece, Eleanor Despenser, née de Clare (older sister of Margaret and Elizabeth), who was also the wife of his powerful and despotic chamberlain and favourite, Hugh Despenser the Younger. Two chroniclers, as well as various entries in Edward's household accounts, make it apparent that the summer of 1326 in Britain was terribly hot; there was a drought, rivers dried up and fires burst out in towns and abbeys owing to the dryness. On 11 July 1326 the king and his niece enjoyed an alfresco picnic in the park of Windsor Castle, and two weeks later when sailing on the Thames not far from Windsor, he ordered a local man to bring him fresh water from a well. Both these events are probably further indications of the heat in the last summer of Edward II's reign.

Windsor Castle, still a royal residence more than 700 years after King Edward III was born there, is within easy reach of London by car and by public transport and is a must-see on the itineraries of many visitors to Britain. It attracts more than half a million visitors annually.

Stirling Castle and the Battlefield of Bannockburn: Edward's Great Defeat

Much of Edward II's reign was taken up by his attempts – failed attempts – to defeat Robert Bruce, who had himself been crowned king of Scotland in 1306. Edward had been raised to believe that he was the rightful overlord of Scotland and that the Scottish kings owed him, and other kings of England, homage for their kingdom. For the first few years of his reign, Robert Bruce had been canny enough to avoid meeting Edward in battle; the king of England, ruler of a much larger and wealthier kingdom, could put a much bigger army in the field than the king of Scotland could. Edward II spent the period from November 1310 to September 1311 at Berwick-upon-Tweed in the far north of his kingdom, trying, and failing, to engage Bruce in battle; he achieved nothing. He finally returned to the south of England in September 1311, and was forced to consent to forty-one wide-ranging reforms of his household and government called the Ordinances. The murder of Piers Gaveston in June 1312 was another matter which distracted Edward's attention from Scotland, and on a happier note, so was the birth of his son and heir, Edward of Windsor, that November.

Robert Bruce and his allies, notably James Douglas and Thomas Randolph, took advantage of the king of England's absence to spend much of 1312 and 1313 capturing castles in Scotland held in English hands, such as Edinburgh, Roxburgh and Perth. They razed them to the ground to prevent Edward II recapturing them. In June 1313, Robert Bruce's only surviving brother Edward Bruce (their other three brothers had been executed by Edward I in 1306/07 in Carlisle and Berwick-upon-Tweed) began besieging the great stronghold of Stirling Castle. Stirling was the key to Scotland; the castle controlled the crossing over the river Forth and thus access to the northern Lowlands and the Highlands. Its constable, Sir Philip Mowbray, made a deal with Edward Bruce that if Edward II did not come to relieve the siege within a year and a day, he would surrender it to Bruce.

This was a challenge even Edward II could not ignore, and so in June 1314 he marched north with the largest army ever raised in England, comprising 15,000 to 20,000 men. Such was the disastrous state of Edward's relations with his earls, however, that only three of them accompanied him: his nephew Gloucester, his brother-in-law Hereford, and his cousin Pembroke. Numerous English magnates and knights, however, did ride north with the king, as did knights from all over Europe seeking glory on the battlefield, Welsh archers, Irish soldiers and some of Robert Bruce's Scottish enemies including Sir John Comyn, whose father John 'the Red' Comyn had been murdered by Bruce in 1306.

Edward II's nephew-in-law and future favourite Hugh Despenser the Younger also fought at Bannockburn. Arrogance and over-confidence was a huge problem on the English side; Edward II took with him a vast baggage train of 216 carts drawn by 424 horses and 880 oxen, supposedly stretching back 20 leagues, which included jewellery, napery, costly plate, and ecclesiastical vestments for celebrating his certain victory.

Edward II did not fight on the first day of the battle of Bannockburn near Stirling Castle, Sunday, 23 June 1314, a series of skirmishes which went the way of the Scots. The earls of Gloucester and Hereford, respectively constable of the army and constable of England, quarrelled over who should command the vanguard; Gloucester was unhorsed during a clash, and Hereford's cousin Henry de Bohun was killed by Robert Bruce himself, who cleaved Bohun's head in with his battle-axe. The advance party of Edward's army, led by the lords Robert Clifford and Henry Beaumont, sustained heavy losses against the schiltrons of Sir Thomas Randolph. Schiltrons were formations consisting of a few hundred men in concentric rings, kneeling by pikes facing outwards. The pikes were about 14 to 18ft long with a sharpened steel point, and positioned at the height of a horse's neck or chest. Schiltrons can be visualised as a forest of pikes sticking out in every direction and were extremely effective against knights charging at them on horseback – as long as the men holding them kept their nerve and did not break and run at the sight of hundreds of men in armour on hundreds of large horses galloping full tilt straight at them with lances outstretched.

The following morning, 24 June 1314, Edward's 23-year-old nephew Gilbert de Clare, earl of Gloucester, rode at the Scottish lines without waiting for an order to advance. He and his horse, and his men following behind him, ran into one of the schiltrons full on, and the young earl was killed. Many of his men died too, as the rest of the vanguard, following closely behind, failed to pull up in time and crashed into Gloucester's men, pushing them onto the long, sharp pikes. The English cavalry advanced towards the schiltrons, but were unable to make headway against the deadly forest of stakes, and those behind, unable to see what was happening, pushed the men in front into range of the lethal pikes. Dead bodies, of men and horses, piled up before the schiltrons; horses who had lost their riders ran around, adding to the terrible confusion. Within minutes, the battle of Bannockburn slipped beyond Edward II's control.

Edward himself, showing great courage and foolhardiness, was right in the thick of the mêlée, attacking ferociously 'like a lioness deprived of her cubs', according to one chronicler. At one point, his horse was killed beneath him, and Scottish soldiers rushed forward to capture him. Edward's knights surrounded him, beating them off, and although his shield-bearer was captured, the king managed to mount another horse from the many running around the battlefield. Again, Scottish soldiers pressed forward to try to capture him, and grabbed hold of his horse. Edward lashed out about him with his mace and held them off, but after only an hour or two of fighting he had lost the battle and his cavalry could make no headway against the Scottish pikes. The archers he had brought with him could not shoot their arrows without hitting their own side as well. Edward's cousin, Aymer de Valence, earl of Pembroke, grabbed the reins of the king's horse and dragged him protesting from the battlefield. Edward's remaining there and being captured would have meant that the English would have to pay an unimaginably massive ransom to Robert Bruce for his return, and his death would have brought his 19-month-old son Edward of Windsor to the throne, with all the perils of a very long regency this entailed. The king's departure from the battlefield was, therefore, the only sensible option, however unimpressive it appears in retrospect. Had Edward been a coward, he would not have been fighting in the middle of the battle in the first place, and he was wounded, perhaps quite badly; his queen, Isabella of France, later tended his wounds herself. After his departure his army broke up and fled, and supposedly the Bannockburn stream could be crossed with dry feet, such were the numbers of dead men lying in it. The king of England sought refuge inside Stirling Castle, but its constable refused, for Edward's own safety, to admit him, pointing out that he could be trapped and besieged there and would not be able to escape. Edward therefore had to gallop hard the almost 70 miles to Dunbar on the coast.

Edward's enormous baggage train and privy seal had to be left behind, though Robert Bruce courteously returned the seal to him. Edward's brother-in-law, Humphrey de Bohun, earl of Hereford – one of the men who had killed Piers Gaveston near Warwick Castle two years earlier – was captured at Bannockburn. In exchange for Hereford and various other English noblemen, Edward II had to release all the Scottish hostages in England, including Robert Bruce's wife Elizabeth de Burgh, who had been held under house arrest since 1306, Bruce's sisters Christina and

Mary, his daughter Marjorie, and his nephew Donald of Mar (who in fact was so close to Edward II that he voluntarily remained in England until Edward's downfall in late 1326). For the rest of Edward II's reign, the battle of Bannockburn was called the 'discomfiture at Strivelyn', the fourteenth-century name for Stirling. It was not generally known as the 'battle of Bannockburn' in Edward's own lifetime, though the author of the fourteenth-century Middle English *Brut* chronicle referred to the location of the battle as 'Bannokes-born'.

Bannockburn is remembered more than 700 years later as one of England's most humiliating military defeats in history, and is, naturally, remembered with far greater affection in Scotland than it is south of the border. There is now a visitor centre near the site of the battle, about 2 miles south of the town of Stirling. The centre boasts a 3D interpretation centre where visitors can participate in a strategic battle game and watch a demonstration of how the battle was won (and lost). Stirling Castle itself originally dates back to the early 1100s, and was handed over to King Henry II of England as part of the ransom for King William the Lion (r. 1165–1214), whom Henry had captured in 1174. Edward I took Stirling Castle in 1296 but almost immediately lost it again in the aftermath of his army's loss at the battle of Stirling Bridge, nearby; he regained it in 1304 after a long siege and it remained in English hands for the next decade, until his son lost the battle of Bannockburn.

Edward III captured Stirling in 1336, then lost it again to the Scots in 1342. Stirling Castle was a royal home in the fifteenth and sixteenth centuries, and some of the highlights of a visit to Stirling, including the royal palace, the chapel royal and the great hall, date from this time period. It is open every day to visitors except Christmas Day and Boxing Day from 9.30 am until 5 pm (from 1 October to 31 March) or 6 pm. Tickets can be bought in advance online. The town of Stirling is situated about 40 miles from Edinburgh and 30 from Glasgow, and its well preserved old town is also well worth a visit, quite apart from the castle.

Dunbar Castle, East Lothian, Scotland: Edward's Refuge after Bannockburn

Edward II had to ride hard the almost 70 miles to Dunbar Castle following his loss at the battle of Bannockburn. Patrick, earl of Dunbar, although he did not fight for Edward at Bannockburn, was friendly to the English king, and his castle was the nearest point of safety. Robert Bruce's close ally Sir James Douglas pursued Edward and his large bodyguard along the Firth of Forth, past Falkirk, Linlithgow and Edinburgh, most of the way to Dunbar on the south-east coast of Scotland. Douglas and his men had little hope of catching Edward, but picked off any stragglers, and it was said that Edward and his bodyguard had no time even to stop and pass water. Edward was surrounded by about 500 knights, among them Hugh Despenser the Younger and Despenser's father, Hugh the Elder, one of his baby son's godfathers. Finally, after a long, hard and desperate gallop which must have taken most of the day, he arrived at the coast. Patrick, earl of Dunbar, opened up the drawbridge of Dunbar Castle for him, and the king was led inside to safety. Edward later granted one William le Franceis (whose name means 'the Frenchman') a very generous income of 50 marks (£33) annually in gratitude for the unspecified 'kind service he lately performed for the king in his presence at Dunbar'.

Earl Patrick commandeered a fishing boat, and the king of England, one of the most powerful men in Europe, was forced to use it to sail down the coast to the port of Berwick-upon-Tweed, with a handful of attendants. Both he and, probably, just about everyone else in Europe had assumed that he could not lose a battle to Robert Bruce, but instead of returning to England at the head of a victorious army, Edward II slipped back into his kingdom in a fishing boat. It must have been the greatest humiliation of his life. To make matters even worse, Edward must have been aware that his father had captured Dunbar Castle in April 1296, while he himself only ever saw it in headlong flight from a battle he had contrived to lose. Earl Patrick of Dunbar, who was born c. 1285 and was almost exactly Edward II's own age, soon afterwards came to terms with Robert Bruce, switched sides, and helped Robert take the port of Berwick-upon-Tweed from Edward in 1318. Patrick lived a remarkably long life; he was still alive in 1368.

The town of Dunbar is 30 miles east of Edinburgh and also 30 miles from Berwick-upon-Tweed, detailed elsewhere in this volume. The ancient site has perhaps been fortified for thousands of years, and the origins of the castle are unknown but may date back to the seventh century. A man who fought for Robert Bruce at Bannockburn and who was his close relative and faithful follower for many years was Thomas Randolph, earl of Moray (d. 1332). Thomas's daughter Agnes, called 'Black Agnes', was as redoubtable as he was. She married Patrick, earl of Dunbar, who was decades her senior, and successfully held Dunbar Castle against a siege led by the English nobleman William Montacute, earl of Salisbury, which lasted for five months in 1338. Dunbar Castle, being in an important strategic position, was attacked, besieged, captured, slighted, rebuilt and re-fortified numerous times throughout the Middle Ages. Mary, Queen of Scots (r. 1542 – 67, executed 1587) often visited Dunbar, and was taken there by her third husband, Lord Bothwell, in 1567 after he abducted her.

The few remaining ruins of Dunbar Castle – part of its gatehouse and walls – are not open to the public, but can easily be seen from the harbour which they overlook, and from the beach (at low tide). Information boards narrate the long history of the site and its castle.

Tonbridge Castle, Kent: Seized by Edward's Nephew-in-Law

Tonbridge Castle was built shortly after the Norman Conquest by Richard FitzGilbert, who was often known as 'Richard of Tonbridge' or 'Richard of Clare' from his landholdings (the village of Clare is located in Suffolk). His descendants used the name 'de Clare' which means 'of Clare', and were one of the greatest noble families in England in the Middle Ages. Gilbert 'the Red' de Clare (b. 1243), earl of Gloucester and Hertford, married Edward II's sister Joan of Acre on 30 April 1290, and they had four children: Gilbert the younger, Eleanor, Margaret and Elizabeth, born between 1291 and 1295. Tonbridge Castle and all the other vast estates belonging to Gilbert 'the Red' in England, Wales and Ireland passed to Edward II's nephew Gilbert de Clare the younger, earl of Gloucester and Hertford, who was only seven years his uncle's junior. His father's vast inheritance made the young earl the third richest man in the kingdom after Edward II and Edward's first cousin, Thomas of Lancaster, earl of Lancaster and Leicester. The earl of Gloucester was killed at Bannockburn in June 1314, and as his widow Maud, one of the many daughters of the Anglo-Irish magnate the earl of Ulster, claimed to be pregnant (she was not), Tonbridge Castle was taken into the king's hands, as were all of Gloucester's estates in England, Wales and Ireland.

Gloucester's three joint and equal heirs were his sisters: Eleanor, wife of Hugh Despenser the Younger; Margaret, widow of Piers Gaveston;

and Elizabeth, widow of the earl of Ulster's eldest son John de Burgh. Edward II, however, who wished to keep his nephew's lands and enormous income in his own hands for as long as possible, pretended for almost three years that Maud de Clare was going to bear her late husband's posthumous child, and refused to partition the lands among his three nieces. Hugh Despenser the Younger, husband of the eldest sister Eleanor, grew angry as he desperately wanted his share of his late brother-in-law's income. On or a little before 20 May 1315, eleven months after the earl of Gloucester fell at Bannockburn, Despenser, along with a motley crew of knights and adventurers, took matters into his own hands and seized the castle of Tonbridge. Edward II was at Hadleigh in Essex when he heard of the 'outrage', as he called it, and sent his escheator John Abel to take possession of Tonbridge Castle. Despenser and his men raised the drawbridge against Abel and refused to let him in, but almost as soon as Abel had left, Despenser gave up possession of the castle and rode the 40 miles to Edward II to explain himself in person. He was never punished for his illegal seizure of Tonbridge.

By seizing control of the castle, Hugh Despenser the Younger was not trying to keep hold of it, but was making a point; almost certainly, he simply wanted the king to admit that the dowager countess of Gloucester could not be pregnant by her husband eleven months after his death. The king still refused, and even at the end of 1316 continued to pretend that Countess Maud would bear a 'living boy' to her dead husband, and that the earl of Gloucester's lands were in his hands because of 'the minority of the heir'. It was only in May 1317, two years after Hugh Despenser the Younger's escapade at Tonbridge Castle and just under three years after the earl of Gloucester's death, that Edward II ordered the partition of his late nephew's vast lands to begin. Although the king became infatuated with Hugh Despenser in later years, in 1315/16 he still disliked and distrusted him, and seemed to enjoy thwarting him. Despenser had a low income by the standards of his own class, only £200 a year (by way of comparison, his late brother-in-law the earl of Gloucester's annual income had been close to £7,000 and Piers Gaveston's was £4,000) and was desperate for the revenues of his wife's share of the de Clare inheritance.

The de Clare lands were finally ready to be partitioned in November 1317. The manor and castle of Tonbridge were given to Hugh Despenser the Younger's sister-in-law Margaret, second of the earl of Gloucester's three sisters and widow of Piers Gaveston, and her new husband Sir Hugh Audley, a knight of the royal household and the second son of an Oxfordshire baron. The couple subsequently spent most of their time living at Tonbridge Castle. Hugh Audley, influential at court between 1315 and 1317 – and perhaps a lover of the king – later turned against Edward II, and fought against the royal army at the battle of Boroughbridge in Yorkshire (see below) in March 1322. He was imprisoned, though escaped in late 1325 or 1326, and joined Edward II's wife Isabella when she returned to England at the head of an invasion force in September 1326 intending to bring Hugh Despenser the Younger down. Audley's wife Margaret, meanwhile, once high in her uncle the king's favour, was sent to Sempringham Priory in Lincolnshire with their toddler daughter, Margaret the younger, in May 1322 and remained there until December 1326, after the king and Hugh Despenser the Younger's downfall. During the years of Despenser's dominance of the English government between 1322 and 1326, he and the king often stayed at Tonbridge Castle; Edward II was there in April and June 1324, and Despenser in September and October 1325 with his pregnant wife Eleanor. On his visit here in June 1324, the unconventional Edward II borrowed a boat from a local fisherman to go fishing, presumably on the River Medway.

Tonbridge Castle was besieged in 1088 not long after it was built during a rebellion against William the Conqueror's son and successor King William II, 'Rufus', and was besieged again in 1264 by Edward II's grandfather Henry III during the baronial wars of that decade. Edward I succeeded his father Henry III as king while on crusade in the Holy Land in November 1272, and on Edward and Queen Leonor's return to England in August 1274, Gilbert 'the Red' de Clare entertained them at Tonbridge shortly before they were crowned as king and queen of England at Westminster Abbey on 19 August. Gilbert became the royal couple's son-in-law on 30 April 1290 when, at the age of 46, he married his second wife, their daughter, Joan of Acre. Joan's little brother Edward of Caernarfon was present at their wedding, five days after his sixth birthday. The newlyweds Gilbert and Joan left court without permission soon afterwards and went to Tonbridge Castle, much to the king's annoyance; he temporarily confiscated some of Joan's goods as punishment. Edward I went on campaign on the Continent against Philip IV of France in the summer of 1297, and left 13-year-old Edward of Caernarfon as nominal regent of his kingdom in his absence; the boy stayed at Tonbridge Castle with members of a regency council appointed to guide and advise him in his role as 'keeper of the realm'.

After the death of Edward II's nephew-in-law Hugh Audley (made earl of Gloucester in 1337 by Edward III) in November 1347, the castle passed to Audley's only child Margaret and her husband Ralph Stafford, made first earl of Stafford in 1351. The Stafford family, who owned Tonbridge Castle for generations, became dukes of Buckingham in the fifteenth century. Henry Stafford, duke of Buckingham, was beheaded by Richard III in 1483, and his son Edward Stafford by Henry VIII in 1521.

Some ruins of the castle still survive, notably the thirteenth-century gatehouse and the great hall, and stand in a public park in the centre of the town of Tonbridge. The castle is open every day except Christmas and New Year, and the grounds are always open to the public for free during daylight hours. The Chamber Room, gatehouse and great hall can be booked for events and ceremonies, including weddings (civil ceremonies only). The town of Tonbridge lies 30 miles from London and 40 from Canterbury, and there is a railway station.

The Fens, near Cambridge, and Ely Cathedral: Edward Goes on Holiday

Ely Cathedral, 16 miles from the city of Cambridge, is often known as the Ship of the Fens. It stands on one of the few hills to be found in this very flat part of eastern England known as the Fens, a naturally marshy region of over 200 square miles which was drained in the eighteenth and early nineteenth centuries. The Fens cover parts of the counties of Norfolk, Cambridgeshire and Lincolnshire, and a small part of Suffolk. The area, when it was marshland, provided an excellent hiding-place; Hereward the Wake, leader of the English resistance to William the Conqueror after 1066, hid in the Fens, and William built a castle in Cambridge as a base for dealing with Hereward and his allies.

In Edward II's time (and long before and after) the Fens and other low-lying areas of eastern England were malarial, and when he was nine in 1293 Edward came down with malaria, or the 'tertian fever' or 'quartan fever' as it was then called, after visiting the area. He spent a congenial month in the Fens in September/October 1315 when he was 31, fifteen months after his defeat at the battle of Bannockburn, on holiday with what a baffled and contemptuous chronicler called 'a great company of common people'. Edward passed the time swimming and rowing at King's Lynn in Norfolk and at Fen Ditton and Impington near Cambridge in what was one of the wettest years of the fourteenth century, perhaps even of the entire Middle Ages. The contemporary author of the Westminster chronicle *Flores Historiarum* or 'Flowers of History', Edward II's most vicious critic, sneered at the king's holiday, saying sarcastically that Edward went to the Fens to 'refresh his soul with many waters', a perfectly normal thing to do in later centuries but very strange to the fourteenth-century mind. Edward was, as indeed he was in many ways, hundreds of years ahead of his time; today many people enjoy sailing along the Fen waterways, and swimming remains an immensely popular leisure activity. In February 1303 when Edward was 18 and Prince of Wales, he went swimming in the River Thames at Windsor. The water, given the time of year, must have been bitterly cold. The Prince had to pay a few shillings compensation to his Fool, Robert Bussard, for playing 'a trick on him in the water'. This is just one of several examples of Edward II's fondness for swimming, and he evidently loved spending time by water.

Edward often visited Ely Cathedral in his youth and again in adulthood. He spent Easter Sunday in the year 1314 (which fell on 7 April) there, just a few weeks before he headed north to his catastrophic defeat at the battle of Bannockburn. St Albans Abbey in Hertfordshire, where Edward had just come from, possessed the body of St Alban, the first British Christian martyr who probably died in the early fourth century, exactly 1,000 years before Edward's time. Ely Cathedral owned a reliquary which they also claimed to be St Alban's. A curious Edward ordered the Ely monks to open the reliquary, stating:

> You know that my brothers of St Albans believe that they possess the body of the martyr. In this place the monks say that they have the body of the same saint. By God's soul, I want to see in which place I ought chiefly to pay reverence to the remains of that holy body.

The holy relics brought a lot of visitors, and revenue, to the cathedral, and the monks were reluctant to open the reliquary, partly out of superstitious dread, and partly because they feared to find it empty and therefore potentially losing lots of revenue from pilgrims. Eventually Edward lifted the lid himself, and found rough cloth spattered with blood, supposedly as fresh as if it had been spilt that very day. He declared that he had seen the clothes the murdered saint had been wearing a millennium earlier, and both he and the monks present fell to their knees at the sight of the miracle. Edward told them on his departure:

> Rejoice in the gift of God, rejoice in the sanctity and merits of so great a martyr; for if, as you say, God does many miracles here by reason of this garment, you may believe that at St Albans he does more, by reason of the most holy body that rests there.

Curiously enough, Edward II's great-grandson Richard II also believed that he witnessed a miracle at Ely Cathedral seventy years later. During a royal visit to the shrine of Walsingham in Norfolk in the early summer of 1383, an accident befell Sir James Berners, a knight of Richard II's chamber and a friend of the king. As the royal party passed through Ely, Berners was struck by lightning during a sudden and violent thunderstorm which supposedly left him blind and half crazed. Richard II, distressed, ordered all the clergy with him to proceed to the shrine of St Etheldreda the Virgin in Ely Cathedral and pray for the inflicted man. When Berners appeared before the shrine in person he saw Etheldreda and St John the Baptist in a vision, and was, so it was told, miraculously cured of his blindness and insanity. A few weeks later, an awed Richard II spoke at length about what he had seen:

> the king saw many wonders wrought by the divine power on the intercession of that glorious virgin, among others in the bestowal of sight upon a knight of the king's, who was blinded by lightning in the night-time, which miracle took place in the king's presence in the company of many persons…

The history of Ely Cathedral dates back to the seventh century and was originally founded as a monastery by St Etheldreda, who supposedly restored Sir James Berners' sight in 1383, in about 672. Etheldreda's shrine stood in Ely for nearly 900 years until 1541, when it was destroyed during the Dissolution of the Monasteries. The present cathedral was begun in 1083, and construction took hundreds of years. In February 1322, during Edward II's reign and eight years after he opened St Alban's reliquary in the cathedral, Ely's central tower collapsed. Edward's master carpenter William Hurley was one of the men who worked on the rebuilding and on the central octagonal tower which exists to this day and is a masterpiece of engineering (Hurley also worked on Caerphilly Castle at the request of Edward II's nephew-in-law and favourite Hugh Despenser the Younger in the mid-1320s; see below). The magnificent Lady Chapel of Ely Cathedral was begun in 1321 and took thirty years to build, and during the Reformation 200 years later, the heads of all the statues in the chapel were either hacked off or defaced.

Ely Cathedral is open to visitors daily, and payment of an admission fee is requested as the building costs £6,000 every day to maintain. The fee includes a guided tour. The town of Ely is also an interesting place to visit, and close to the cathedral is the home of Oliver Cromwell, Lord Protector of England after the Civil War, who moved there in 1636 (he was born in nearby Huntingdon in 1599). Ely lies just a few miles from Cambridge and can be reached by train from there in under twenty minutes, and is 80 miles north of London and 30 from Peterborough.

If you visit the Fens, you can do what Edward II did in the autumn of 1315 by sailing along the waterways in a hired narrowboat, and the area is home to 25 per cent of Britain's rarest wildlife and thirteen globally rare species. The Fens' unofficial capital is the town of Wisbech, Cambridgeshire, which makes a great base for exploring the area. Peterborough, 30 miles from Ely, is a convenient station if you are travelling to the Fens by train, and the ancient university city of Cambridge is full of medieval buildings and other treasures and is an absolute must-see. The city is also associated with Edward II as he founded a university college here in 1317 (see elsewhere in this volume). Edward spent part of his 1315 holiday at Impington, a village just to the north of Cambridge; he also stayed in Fen Ditton 4 miles from Impington, also just outside the city of Cambridge.

Eltham Palace, Kent: Birthplace of Edward's Second Son

When he was 21 years old in 1305, Edward of Caernarfon, Prince of Wales, received a generous gift from Anthony Bek (d. 1311), bishop of Durham and the only Englishman in history to hold the title 'patriarch of Jerusalem': his palace of Eltham in Kent. (The generous Bek also gave

Somerton Castle in Lincolnshire to Edward four years later.) Edward in turn gave Eltham to his queen Isabella of France, in October 1311, possibly in gratitude for her support of Piers Gaveston, who had just been banished from England for the third time and whom the queen appears to have been aiding financially. Edward and Isabella stayed at Eltham from 15 to 20 February 1308, just days after the queen's arrival in England and shortly before their coronation at Westminster Abbey.

Queen Isabella gave birth to her and Edward's second son, John of Eltham, at Eltham Palace on 15 August 1316. It would have been conventional by the standards of the time for the queen to have named her second son Philip after her father King Philip IV of France (d. November 1314), but for some reason she did not. Instead, she chose the name John. This was the name of Edward II's great-grandfather King John (d. 1216) and of his eldest brother, who died at the age of 5 in 1271, thirteen years before Edward was even born, and almost a quarter of a century before Isabella herself was. It seems most likely, however, that Isabella named her child in honour of the new pope, John XXII, whose birth name was Jacques Duèse and who, prior to his election, was cardinal-bishop of Porto. John was elected pope by a conclave of cardinals in Lyon, France, on 7 August 1316, and the news reached England in mid-August 1316 exactly at the time of little John of Eltham's birth. Edward II was 200 miles away in York in August 1316, the only time he was not close by when his and Isabella's children were born, and he gave a very large gift of £100 to Isabella's messenger for bringing him the news. The St Albans chronicler reports on the 'joy' the king felt at the birth of his second son. On 24 August 1316, just after hearing the news, Edward asked the Dominican friars of York to pray for the well-being of himself, his wife and their two sons Edward of Windsor and John of Eltham, 'especially on account of John'.

It was usual for fourteenth-century English royals to be known by their birthplaces, and the young John was always called 'Lord John of Eltham'. He was 10 years old when his father was forced to abdicate his throne to his elder son, John's 14-year-old brother Edward of Windsor, in January 1327, and most probably attended his father's funeral at St Peter's Abbey in Gloucestershire in December that year. During his childhood, John of Eltham was sometimes looked after by his much older first cousin Eleanor, Lady Despenser, née de Clare, who, despite being twenty-four years his senior, was also a grandchild of Edward I. John of Eltham was made earl of Cornwall at a parliament held in Salisbury in October 1328 early in his brother's reign, and died in Scotland in September 1336 at the age of only 20, unmarried and childless. His tomb in Westminster Abbey still exists; see also below under 'Westminster Abbey'.

Little is known about Eltham Palace before Anthony Bek gave it to Edward of Caernarfon in 1305, but apparently Bek himself had it built in the late thirteenth century. Eltham Palace is still lived in today, and was a favourite residence of many of the English kings in the fourteenth and fifteenth centuries. Edward II's son Edward III had Eltham renovated in the 1350s and 1360s, and Edward III's grandson Henry IV often stayed at Eltham. In late 1400 and early 1401, he hosted the Byzantine emperor Manuel Palaiologus here. Manuel, seeking the aid of western Christian rulers against the Ottoman forces attacking his capital of Constantinople (which became Istanbul after it fell to the Ottomans in 1453), was the only reigning Byzantine emperor who ever set foot in England. The Great Hall of Eltham which exists today, with its elaborate oak roof, was built by Edward IV (r. 1461–83) in the 1470s, and he remodelled much of the palace (Edward IV was Edward II and Isabella of France's great-great-great-grandson via one line, and great-great-great-great-great-grandson via another). Henry VIII (r. 1509–47), Edward IV's grandson and the second of the Tudor kings, grew up at Eltham in the 1490s and beginning of the 1500s, and met the great scholar Erasmus here in 1499.

Eltham was sacked by parliamentary troops during the Civil War of the 1640s, and fell into decline. By the eighteenth century, the ruins had become a farm and the great hall was used as a barn. Stephen and Virginia Courtauld leased the site in the 1930s, and built an Art Deco house next to the ruins of the fifteenth-century great hall. Eltham Palace is now looked after by English Heritage and its extensive gardens are open most days of the year and, as with a few other buildings in Britain associated with Edward II, it can now be hired for weddings and other events. It is located in the borough of Greenwich in south-east London, and can easily be reached by car, bus or train.

St Andrew's Church, Heckington, Lincolnshire: Likeness of a King

In the Lincolnshire village of Heckington, 23 miles south of Lincoln, 12 miles west of Boston, 30 miles north of Stamford and 33 miles north of Peterborough, is a church built in Edward II's reign and strongly associated with Edward's chaplain Richard Potesgrave, whose tomb lies in the church to this day. The church of St Andrew is a wonderful example of fourteenth-century ecclesiastical architecture and of the Decorated style of medieval English Gothic, and is decorated inside and out with many fine stone carvings of faces, beasts, gargoyles, angels and animals. One such head, on the outside of the church, almost certainly represents Edward II himself; it shows a crowned man with a beard, and bears a strong resemblance to other fourteenth-century depictions of Edward, for example his tomb effigy in Gloucester Cathedral, a stone corbel in the great hall of Caerphilly Castle, and a carving of him in a church in Winchelsea, Sussex.

The patrons of St Andrew's Church, the family who owned the manor of Heckington in the fourteenth century, were the Beaumonts. Henry, Lord Beaumont and titular earl of Buchan in Scotland (c. 1270/80–1340), who probably had the nave of St Andrew's built, was a second cousin of Edward II, and was a French nobleman by birth. His mother, Agnes Beaumont, was Viscountess of Beaumont-au-Maine in France; Henry and several of his siblings took their mother's name. His father, Louis Brienne, sometimes also called Louis of Acre, was the son of John Brienne, the king of Jerusalem, Latin emperor of Constantinople and claimant to the throne of Armenia. Henry Beaumont was a close ally of his kinsman Edward II for much of his reign and fought for him at the battle of Bannockburn in June 1314; they fell out in 1323 when Edward made a thirteen-year peace treaty with Scotland. Beaumont claimed the earldom of Buchan by right of his wife Alice Comyn (d. 1349), niece and co-heir of John Comyn, earl of Buchan (d. 1308); if England and Scotland made a peace settlement, Beaumont would never be able to claim the earldom and its lands. He joined Edward's queen Isabella, after her invasion of September 1326, but later turned against her too when she made a permanent peace settlement with Scotland in the summer of 1328. Beaumont fled abroad and plotted an invasion of England in July/August 1330. He returned to England after Edward III overthrew his mother Isabella in October 1330 and began ruling his own kingdom, and via his daughter Isabella, Duchess of Lancaster (c. 1315/18–1359/60), Henry Beaumont was the great-grandfather of King Henry IV.

Richard Potesgrave, Edward II's chaplain and the man responsible for building the chancel of St Andrew's, was appointed as one of the men responsible for guarding Edward II's body in St Peter's Abbey, Gloucester, between 20 October and 20 December 1327. Edward had reportedly died at Berkeley Castle in Gloucestershire on 21 September 1327, and the news was taken to his young son Edward (not yet 15 years old) in Lincoln by Sir Thomas Gurney, a knight of Somerset. Whether Edward II was truly dead is not completely certain, as many influential men including his own half-brother the earl of Kent and the archbishop of York plotted to free him in 1329/30 and were profoundly convinced that he was still alive, and it seems as though the body was sealed in its coffin and that no one, not even his son the king, had the chance to see him (see also below under 'Gloucester Cathedral').

St Andrew's Church, Heckington, is well worth a visit for anyone in the Lincolnshire/Cambridgeshire area, being a splendid example of fourteenth-century ecclesiastical architecture with dozens of wonderful stone carvings, and a gorgeously-carved Easter Sepulchre and sedilla also from the fourteenth century. Guided tours of the church are available.

Somerton Castle, near Lincoln: Given to Edward

Somerton Castle, just south of Lincoln near the villages of Boothby Graffoe, Coleby and Navenby (and 18 miles from Heckington), once belonged to Edward II personally. It was given to him in August 1309 by Anthony Bek, bishop of Durham and patriarch of Jerusalem. (The same man who generously gave Edward his palace of Eltham in Kent in 1305.) Bek had built Somerton in the 1280s, and Edward II sometimes stayed there when he was on his way to Lincoln or holding parliament there. His son Edward III imprisoned his first cousin Margaret, countess of Norfolk in her own right (c. 1322–99), at Somerton Castle in 1354 after she left England without his permission to try to persuade the pope to annul her first marriage to John, Lord Segrave, and after she married her second husband Sir Walter Manny also without his permission. Not long afterwards, Somerton Castle also served as a prison for King John II of France, captured at the battle of Poitiers in 1356 by Edward III's eldest son Edward of Woodstock, the legendary 'Black Prince'. John was imprisoned here from 1359 to 1360, 'imprisoned' in the loosest sense of the word as he was treated with the utmost honour and respect and had a large retinue befitting his rank. King John was, however, never released as his subjects were never able to pay his ransom, and died in England in April 1364.

Another unhappy event associated with Somerton Castle in the fourteenth century involved the great noblewoman Alice de Lacy (1281–1348), who inherited the earldom of Lincoln from her father Henry de Lacy (d. 1311) and the earldom of Salisbury from her mother Margaret Longespee (d. c. 1306/08). Alice married Edward II's first cousin Thomas, earl of Lancaster, in 1294, but left him in 1317, possibly with Edward II's help and support, and they were estranged for the remaining five years of Thomas's life. Even so, Thomas's very existence protected Alice, and his execution on the orders of Edward II in March 1322 left her vulnerable; she was forced to hand over some of her rich estates to the king and Hugh Despenser the Younger, and to acknowledge a huge debt to him. Alice married her second husband Sir Eble Lestrange in 1324, and it seems to have been a genuine love-match; the couple lived quietly for the remaining years of Edward II's reign and the first few years of Edward III's. Eble died in September 1335, and Alice was living at Bolingbroke Castle in Lincolnshire, part of her own inheritance, later that year (or early in 1336) when she was abducted by Sir Hugh de Frene with the connivance of some of her own servants and her half-brother John de Lacy, a clerk in her household. Frene, a rather obscure knight, took Alice the 30 miles to Somerton Castle, and married her there against her will. He subsequently took her to the Tower of London and kept her there in close confinement. Alice petitioned Edward III describing her appalling experience, but Frene suffered no punishment for his act, though he did not have long to enjoy Alice's wealth as he died on campaign in Scotland a few months later. He was probably decades Alice's junior, but she outlived him by eleven years. A born survivor, she finally died in October 1348 at the age of almost 67.

Somerton Castle passed from Edward II to his son Edward, who spent £200 renovating it in the mid-1330s, and it remained in royal ownership until sold by Charles I in 1628. By 1601 the castle was in a ruinous state, and still was in the eighteenth century. In the nineteenth it was converted into a farmhouse and is still inhabited today; what remains of the medieval castle Edward II would have known is incorporated into the building, and part of the medieval moat is still there. A Grade I Listed building, it is privately owned and not open to the public, though can be seen from the road; the nearby church of All Saints in Coleby is also well worth a trip for anyone visiting the area. One of its rectors was Thomas Cantilupe (d. 1282), who became Bishop of Hereford on the other side of the country in 1275 and was also lord chancellor of England and chancellor of the University of Oxford. Cantilupe was canonised as a saint in 1320 by Pope John XXII (1316–34) during Edward II's reign, thanks in large part to Edward's own efforts; he sent John XXII and his predecessor Clement V (1305–14) numerous letters promoting Cantilupe's sainthood. Cantilupe was the last Englishman to be made a saint before the Reformation.

Dunstanburgh Castle, Northumberland: Built by Edward's Cousin and Enemy

Standing grandly on the north-east coast of England is the ruined castle of Dunstanburgh, built by Edward II's first cousin and enemy Thomas of Lancaster, earl of Lancaster and Leicester. Thomas was born at the end of 1277 or beginning of 1278, and was the eldest son of Edward I's younger brother Edmund, earl of Lancaster and Leicester (1245–96) and his second wife Blanche of Artois (1245/8–1302), niece of King Louis IX of France. Thomas of Lancaster was the son, brother and uncle of queens, and the grandson, nephew and uncle of kings. He was by far the most royal of the English earls in Edward II's reign, and by far the richest. As his long but unhappy marriage to Alice de Lacy, countess of Lincoln, produced no surviving children, Thomas's heir was his younger brother Henry (1280/81–1345).

Dunstanburgh lies on a headland near the village of Craster, about 12 miles south of the great castle of Bamburgh, 25 miles south of Lindisfarne or Holy Island, and 40 miles north of Newcastle-upon-Tyne. Thomas of Lancaster's reasons for building the castle are not entirely clear; perhaps he intended it as a rather remote refuge from his cousin the king if necessary, or perhaps as a display of his great wealth and power and of his opposition to Edward II. Edward gave Thomas a 'licence to crenellate' at Dunstanburgh on 28 August 1315, though in fact Thomas's accounts reveal that he had begun to build the castle more than two years before receiving official permission from the king to do so.

According to one very pro-Lancastrian fourteenth-century chronicler, Thomas and his baronial allies, enemies of the king, decided to flee from his home of Pontefract in Yorkshire to Dunstanburgh in March 1322, where they would wait until the king's anger with them had burned itself out. The plan failed and Thomas was executed at Pontefract shortly

Caernarfon Castle, Gwynedd, North Wales: Edward II's birthplace on 25 April 1284 when it was in the earliest stages of construction.

The Eagle Tower, Caernarfon Castle, traditionally Edward's birthplace.

A statue of Edward II on the King's Gate, Caernarfon Castle, dating to around 1320 in his own lifetime.

Caerlaverock Castle, Dumfries and Galloway, Scotland, scene of Edward's first military experience in July 1300, aged 16.

Lanercost Priory, Cumbria, where Edward spent a few months with his father in 1306/7 and where his father physically attacked him over his relationship with Piers Gaveston.

Knaresborough Castle, Yorkshire. Edward gave the castle to Piers Gaveston in 1307, stayed here several times throughout his reign including in 1307, 1309, 1312 and 1323, and built the keep.

Ruins of Berkhamsted Castle, Hertfordshire. It belonged to Edward's stepmother Queen Marguerite and later to his wife Queen Isabella. Edward witnessed the wedding of his niece Margaret de Clare and Piers Gaveston here in November 1307.

Scarborough Castle, Yorkshire, where Edward left Piers Gaveston in May 1312; Gaveston was besieged there for nine days.

Windsor Castle, Berkshire. Edward's son and heir the future King Edward III was born here on 13 November 1312.

Right: A stone head almost certainly representing Edward II outside St Andrew's Church, Heckington, Lincolnshire, built by Edward's chaplain.

Below: Dunstanburgh Castle, Northumberland, built in the 1310s by Edward's first cousin and greatest enemy Thomas, earl of Lancaster, whom he had beheaded in 1322.

Leeds Castle, Kent. Edward's mother Leonor of Castile owned and much improved this fairy-tale castle built on two islands in a lake. Edward besieged it in October 1321 and subsequently hanged 13 members of the garrison.

Pickering Castle, Yorkshire, was forfeited by Edward's cousin Thomas of Lancaster after his execution in March 1322, and Edward renovated and improved it in 1323.

Rievaulx Abbey, Yorkshire, founded 1132. Edward was staying here in October 1322 when an invading Scottish force almost captured him, and he had to flee to the coast leaving many of his possessions behind.

A stone corbel in the great hall of Caerphilly Castle, South Wales. Almost certainly it represents Edward II, the crowned and bearded head on the right, and his beloved chamberlain, favourite and nephew-in-law Hugh Despenser the Younger on the left. Crown copyright (2018) Cadw, used with permission.

Kenilworth Castle, Warwickshire. Edward spent much time here between 1324 and 1326, and was held in captivity here from early December 1326 until early April 1327. He was forced to abdicate his throne to his teenage son Edward III while at Kenilworth in January 1327.

Berkeley Castle, Gloucestershire; the deposed Edward was sent to Berkeley as a captive in April 1327, and contrary to popular modern myth was well treated here. He supposedly died at Berkeley on 21 September 1327, though the famous 'red-hot poker' narrative of his murder is a myth.

Gloucester Cathedral. Edward II was buried at St Peter's Abbey, now Gloucester Cathedral, on 20 December 1327 three months after his death at Berkeley Castle; his half-brother Edmund, earl of Kent, who attended the funeral, later came to believe that Edward was still alive.

Corfe Castle, Dorset. Edward is strongly associated with Corfe in 1327 after his deposition, and several chroniclers believed that he was imprisoned here. The Fieschi Letter of *c.* 1338 which details Edward's escape from Berkeley Castle and subsequent afterlife in Italy states that he fled to Corfe and lived here for some time.

afterwards, and it is not clear whether he ever even saw his castle at Dunstanburgh. The castle passed to Thomas's brother and heir Henry (d. 1345) and then to his nephew, Henry the younger, and after Henry's death in 1361 to John of Gaunt, second duke of Lancaster, who was both Edward II's grandson and the husband of Thomas's great-niece and heir Blanche of Lancaster (d. 1368). John of Gaunt rebuilt much of what survives at Dunstanburgh today, including converting the massive twin-towered gatehouse into a fortified keep. He and Blanche of Lancaster were the parents of Henry IV, the first Lancastrian king of England.

In the twenty-first century, Dunstanburgh Castle is looked after by English Heritage, and open most days of the week in summer but only at weekends in winter. The great twin-towered gatehouse and keep is ruinous but still most impressive, and the coast around Dunstanburgh and the dramatic sight of its castle ruins make a wonderful location for walks. Visitors can climb the steep steps in the castle's Lilburn Tower and enjoy the views over the sea and up the coast towards Bamburgh Castle. A visit to Dunstanburgh can easily be combined with a visit to Bamburgh, or with a trip to Alnwick Castle 8 miles from Dunstanburgh, the great stronghold of the powerful Percy family in the Middle Ages. Henry, Lord Percy (1273–1314) was one of the men who besieged Piers Gaveston at Scarborough Castle in May 1312, and his grandson Henry, Lord Percy (c. 1320/21–1368), married Thomas of Lancaster's niece Mary of Lancaster (c. 1320/21–1362) in 1334. Mary and Henry's son, born in 1341 and inevitably also called Henry Percy, was made the first earl of Northumberland in 1377. Warkworth Castle, 12 miles south of Dunstanburgh, dates back to the mid-twelfth century, and Edward II spent money on strengthening it in and after 1319. Later in the fourteenth century, it also passed to the Percy family.

Chapter Three

The Last Years, 1317–1326

Trinity College, Cambridge: A Merger of King's Hall, Founded by Edward II in 1317, and Michaelhouse, Founded in 1324

On 7 July 1317, to celebrate the tenth anniversary of his accession to the throne, Edward II founded the King's Hall at Cambridge University as a place to educate the children of his chapel. By the end of 1319, thirty-two scholars lived there, and Edward invited them and their warden to spend that Christmas with him at York. Twenty-six of them arrived late, on 28 December, and one joined in an assault by the prior of the Dominican friars of Pontefract on a local man called William Hardy and was left behind in disgrace when the scholars returned to Cambridge.

Seven years after the foundation of King's Hall, in 1324, Hervey Staunton (or Stanton) founded another college at Cambridge called Michaelhouse. Staunton (d. 1327) was a chief justice of the court of King's Bench, and a staunch supporter of Edward II; when Edward's queen Isabella invaded England in September 1326 intending to bring down Hugh Despenser the Younger, she stole £800 belonging to Staunton which he had stored in Bury St Edmunds, and he died a few months later without ever recovering the money. In 1546, Edward II's descendant Henry VIII merged King's Hall and Michaelhouse to create his new foundation of Trinity College. It seems reasonable, therefore, to acknowledge Edward II and Hervey Staunton as the co-founders, with Henry VIII, of Trinity, arguably the greatest of all Oxbridge colleges. Famous Trinity alumni are too numerous to count, but include Isaac Newton, Niels Bohr, Ludwig Wittgenstein, Lord Byron and six British prime ministers; members of the college have won thirty-two Nobel Prizes. Trinity College is generally open to the public daily, at a small charge.

Edward II also founded Oriel College at Oxford in 1326; see elsewhere in this volume. He was the first of only two people in history to establish colleges at both Oxford and Cambridge, the second being his great-great-great-grandson Henry VI (b. 1421, r. 1422–61 and 1470–71), who founded All Souls at Oxford in 1438, and King's College at Cambridge in 1441. Edward II called the universities of Oxford and Cambridge the 'two special jewels' which enriched his realm in February 1317, a few months before he founded the King's Hall. He is especially important in the history of Cambridge; in March 1317, he asked the pope to recognise its official status as a university, and John XXII duly granted a papal bull to this effect on 9 June 1318. The king also asked John to 'extend and perpetuate the privileges' of the university in March 1318. In 1312 Edward had been involved in the foundation of a university in Dublin, though it did not survive, and at his 1308 foundation of Langley Priory in Hertfordshire, there was a school which prepared students for the universities. The fourteenth century was a great era of Oxbridge college foundations. As well as Edward II's two foundations of King's Hall and Oriel, and Staunton's Michaelhouse in 1324, Edward's ally Walter Stapeldon (d. 1326), Bishop of Exeter and Treasurer of England, founded Exeter College at Oxford in 1314, and his (Edward's) niece Elizabeth de Burgh, née de Clare (1295–1360), founded Clare College, Cambridge in 1338. It was known as Clare Hall until the nineteenth century. Edward II's cousin Marie de St Pol, dowager countess of Pembroke, founded Pembroke College, Cambridge in 1347, originally called the Hall of Valence Marie, and his daughter-in-law Philippa of Hainault (c. 1314–69), queen of Edward III, founded Queen's College, Oxford in 1341 via her chaplain.

The city of Cambridge stands on the River Cam and is the county town of Cambridgeshire. There is a direct train connection from London King's Cross and it can also easily be reached by coach or by car from the M11 motorway. London Stansted airport is just 30 miles away.

Clarendon Palace, Wiltshire:
One of Edward's Residences

Two miles east of Salisbury are the ruins of the medieval palace of Clarendon, where Edward II spent much time in the second half of his reign; he lived there for all of February and March 1317 and for most of August 1326, for example. Edward's cousin and enemy Thomas of Lancaster claimed that while the king was at Clarendon in the spring of 1317, he and his current court favourites, Roger Damory, Hugh Audley and others, hatched a plan to abduct Thomas's wife, Alice de Lacy. Alice, countess of Lincoln and Salisbury in her own right, certainly left Thomas in May 1317 and they lived apart for the remaining five years of Thomas's life, though whether Thomas's suspicions of the king's involvement were correct is unclear.

Also at Clarendon Palace in early 1317, Edward II received a visit from one Brother Nicholas of Wisbech (in Cambridgeshire), formerly the confessor of Edward's sister Margaret, duchess of Brabant. Nicholas came to Edward II at Clarendon with a plan. Edward was in possession of some miraculous holy oil which had once belonged to St Thomas Becket, archbishop of Canterbury (d. 1170), Nicholas said. Why did the king not request pope John XXII's permission to be re-anointed with this holy oil? Doing so would surely end all his political troubles. John XXII did give reluctant permission, but advised Edward to have the ceremony performed in private to avoid scandal. Edward eventually came to his senses and sent the pope a remarkably candid and self-aware letter castigating himself for his own 'imbecility' and 'dove-like simplicity' for allowing himself to be persuaded by the arguments of his sister's confessor. Edward II had ruled England for ten years in 1317, since the death of his father in July 1307; for the most part he had been an utter failure and had lurched from one disaster to another. The author of the *Vita Edwardi Secundi* wrote the following year, 'neither has our King Edward done anything that ought to be preached in the market place or upon the house-tops.' In many ways Edward II was a very likeable man and one whom modern people would probably find considerably easier to relate to on a personal level than most of his predecessors and successors, but he did not have the abilities required to be a successful medieval king.

Edward II stayed at his palace of Clarendon for the last time between 9 and 26 August 1326, during the hot, drought-ridden summer of that year, just a few weeks before the arrival of his wife Isabella's invasion force in Suffolk, which proved to be the beginning of the end of his reign. Always unconventional, and always a lover of the outdoors and physical exercise, Edward joined in when he hired twenty-two men to dig a ditch and make hedges in the park of Clarendon Palace. Working alongside a man called Gibbe (a nickname for Gilbert) in the ditch, the king noticed that Gibbe's shoes were old and in disrepair, and borrowed 12*d* from one of his wheelwrights, Elis Peck, to give to Gibbe so that he could buy himself new shoes. The money was returned to Elis later that day. Such behaviour was entirely typical of Edward II, and it is hard to think of any other medieval king of England who would willingly have jumped into a ditch with a spade or treated labourers as his equals. Edward and his royal predecessors and successors all enjoyed hunting at Clarendon, and hunting was one of the few activities Edward took part in which was, by the standards of medieval royalty, entirely conventional (the others were falconry and breeding horses). In August 1326 he hunted in the park of Clarendon.

It was Edward II's great-great-grandfather, Henry II, who built Clarendon Palace, and passed the Constitutions of Clarendon – sixteen articles limiting ecclesiastical privileges in England – here in 1164. Edward's grandfather, Henry III, rebuilt much of the palace, though by the early fourteenth century it was in much need of repair. Edward ordered an inquisition at Clarendon in 1315 which revealed that the palace had 'numerous defects ... caused by long neglect of roofing'. It also reveals that the king and queen each had their own chambers and chapels at Clarendon, that there was another room called the Antioch Chamber, and that royal children had their own chambers which were connected to the king's chambers by a staircase and a pentice (a covered walkway or porch). There was a large wine cellar, two gates, and walls, ditches, fences and hedges around the palace and its park.

Clarendon Palace was abandoned as a royal residence around the end of the fifteenth century and fell into ruin. Only the east wall of the great hall still stands, though plenty of foundations are also visible, and excavations have revealed much about the impressively large site and the layout of its buildings. The palace site stands on the Clarendon Way, a 25-mile walk connecting the cities of Salisbury and Winchester, and a guided walk to the ruins from Salisbury can be booked; it is 2½ miles on foot from the city centre, and 23 miles from Winchester. Ten miles from Clarendon Palace stood Amesbury Priory, where Edward II's grandmother Eleanor of Provence (c. 1223–91), widow of Henry III and dowager queen of England, retired in 1285, and where Edward's sister Mary of Woodstock (1279–1332), niece Joan Monthermer (fifth and youngest daughter of his sister Joan of Acre), and cousins Eleanor of Brittany and Isabella of Lancaster (d. 1342 and 1348/9 respectively) were nuns. Edward's niece,

Eleanor de Bohun, and great-niece, Joan Gaveston, Piers Gaveston's daughter, grew up at Amesbury though were not veiled as nuns, and his niece Elizabeth de Burgh, née de Clare, gave birth to her daughter Isabella de Verdon at Amesbury on 21 March 1317, eight months after the death of her second husband Theobald de Verdon. Edward's queen, Isabella of France, was escorted to Amesbury from the palace of Clarendon by the under-sheriff of Wiltshire to act as the godmother of little Isabella de Verdon, who was named after her, and Edward himself sent a silver cup as a christening gift. He visited his niece Elizabeth at Amesbury on 10 April 1317 and persuaded her to marry her third husband, his current 'favourite' and perhaps lover, Sir Roger Damory; their wedding took place in his presence at Windsor Castle a few weeks later. Amesbury Priory was closed down during the Dissolution of the Monasteries in Henry VIII's reign and no longer exists, but a seventeenth-century mansion called Amesbury Abbey was built on the site and is now a nursing home (and a Grade I Listed building). Edward of Caernarfon often visited the nearby city of Salisbury throughout his life, including on 2 September 1293 when he was 9 years old and, according to his household clerk, dined there with 'a monk and some other monks'.

Woodstock Palace, Oxfordshire: Birthplace of Edward's First Daughter

Just 8 miles from Oxford stood a great royal palace in the Middle Ages, known as Woodstock Palace. Edward II's elder daughter Eleanor, his and Isabella of France's third child, was born here in June 1318 and was always known as Eleanor of Woodstock in her own lifetime (she was named after her paternal grandmother Leonor (or Eleanor) of Castile). Edward II's half-brother Edmund, earl of Kent, was also born at Woodstock in August 1301, and so, in June 1330, was his grandson Edward, eldest son of Edward III and father of Richard II, and known to posterity as the Black Prince. This, however, is a sixteenth-century appellation, and in his own lifetime he was called Edward of Woodstock.

Woodstock Palace was originally built as a hunting lodge in 1129 by Edward II's great-great-great-great-grandfather Henry I (r. 1100–35), William the Conqueror's youngest son. The king enclosed a park at Woodstock, and kept lions and camels there, as well as the first porcupine seen in England. Henry I's grandson, Henry II (r. 1154–89), rebuilt Woodstock as a palace, and spent much time there with his famous mistress Rosamund Clifford (d. 1176). Most of Edward II's predecessors spent time at Woodstock, as did his successors; his grandfather Henry III entertained his son-in-law Alexander III of Scotland (r. 1249–86) there in 1256, and Edward II's mother Queen Leonor gave birth to her fourth surviving daughter Mary, later a nun at Amesbury Priory, at Woodstock in March 1279. Mary had little if any vocation as a nun, and in the 1310s often visited her brother Edward II's court and went away with lavish gifts. Edward II's great-grandson, Richard II, sometimes stayed at Woodstock, and was there at Christmas 1389 when tragedy struck the royal court; the 17-year-old heir to the earldom of Pembroke, John Hastings, was killed while jousting.

The palace was mostly destroyed by Oliver Cromwell's troops during the Civil War of the 1640s, and between about 1705 and 1722 Blenheim Palace – a gift to John Churchill, first duke of Marlborough, from Queen Anne – was built on the site. Blenheim is open to the public every day of the year except Christmas Day.

Berwick-upon-Tweed, Northumberland: Unsuccessfully Besieged by Edward

The town of Berwick-upon-Tweed lies on the far north-east coast of England just south of the Scottish border, and is the northernmost town in England. In the Middle Ages, it was an important port and changed hands between England and Scotland more than a dozen times, though has been in England since 1482 when the duke of Gloucester, the future King Richard III (r. 1483-85), captured it. Edward II's father Edward I himself captured Berwick in 1296, destroying much of the town and, notoriously, massacring many of the inhabitants. Edward II spent the entire period from early November 1310 to early August 1311 in Berwick; the Lords Ordainer, who had appointed themselves to reform the king's household and government, remained in the south and he wished to avoid them, and hoped to strengthen his position by defeating Robert Bruce in battle. In this aim, he failed utterly.

After Robert Bruce became king of Scotland in 1306, he realised the importance of taking the port of Berwick, and tried on three separate occasions to capture it. Having failed in 1312 and 1316 he succeeded on the third attempt in April 1318, supposedly thanks to the treachery of the Englishman Peter Spalding, who was responsible for a section of the town wall and whom the Scots 'bribed by a great sum of money … and the promise of land', according to two northern chroniclers. Berwick, like everywhere else in Northern Europe, suffered from the terrible effects of the Great Famine in the mid-1310s; between 1314 and 1316 it barely stopped raining, with the result that crops rotted in the fields and up to 10 per cent of the population of England died of hunger and disease. The town of Berwick seems to have suffered particularly badly. Its keeper, Lord Berkeley, told Edward II in 1316 that 'no town was ever in such distress', that the garrison were deserting, dead of hunger or reduced to eating horses, and that if Edward failed to send help immediately 'the town will be lost by famine'. Berkeley ended one letter by saying, 'Pity to see Christians living such a life.'

It was vital for Edward II to recapture Berwick-upon-Tweed from Robert Bruce as soon as possible, but in 1318 he was busy trying to repair his awful relationship with his powerful first cousin Thomas, earl of Lancaster, and it was 1319 before he was able to raise a force in order to besiege Berwick. The campaign should have begun on 10 June 1319, but on 22 May, it was postponed until 22 July. Even then Edward did not arrive in Berwick until 7 September, and although he had a huge force of supposedly around 14,000 men with him (though this contemporary estimate is surely a gross exaggeration), he somehow forgot to take siege-engines. Predictably, Edward's siege of Berwick-upon-Tweed failed completely.

As a decoying tactic, James Douglas and Thomas Randolph, earl of Moray, led an army into England and reached as far south as Boroughbridge, near York. According to a captured Scottish scout, there was a plan to seize Edward's queen Isabella, who was staying at a small manor of the archbishop of York, either Brotherton or Bishopthorpe. The archbishop raised a force of all the men he could find to march out there to protect her, and the queen, surrounded by her bodyguard, hastened to York, from where she escaped by water to the safety of Nottingham. One chronicler even accused Isabella's uncle Thomas, earl of Lancaster, of conspiring with the Scots to capture the queen, and although this is almost certainly untrue, Lancaster left Berwick when his cousin the king threatened to take revenge on him for the death of Piers Gaveston more than seven years before. Edward II raised the siege of Berwick, and marched his army to Northumberland to lie in wait for the Scottish force as they returned home, but they used the western route and eluded him. Edward never again attempted to lay siege to the port of Berwick-upon-Tweed, and it was lost to the English until his son Edward III captured it again in 1333. Berwick was not a happy place as far as Edward II was concerned; he arrived here in June 1314, not at the head of a conquering army but in a fishing boat with a handful of attendants after losing the battle of Bannockburn to Robert Bruce.

One man who took part in the siege of Berwick in 1319 at Edward II's side was Hugh Despenser the Younger (b. c. 1288/89), the man who would bring Edward down in 1326. Despenser had been married to Edward's eldest niece Eleanor de Clare since 1306, but although Edward was extremely fond of Eleanor and of Despenser's father, Hugh the Elder (b. 1261), for many years he ignored Hugh the Younger and seems to have disliked and distrusted him. Despenser was elected as Edward's chamberlain by the English magnates in 1318, and subsequently Edward II's feelings for him underwent a dramatic change. It may be that Despenser seduced Edward and became his lover. This is not certain, but it is beyond doubt that Edward became infatuated with a man he had disliked and distrusted for many years, and in 1326 one abbey annalist called the two men 'the king and his husband'. Queen Isabella also appears to have thought, or known, that the men's relationship was much more than merely friendly, as in a famous speech she made to the French court in late 1325, she accused Despenser of coming between her husband and herself, and of being the third person in her marriage. Chroniclers commented that Despenser had enchanted Edward's mind and that the king loved and trusted him above all others. Hugh Despenser the Younger came to dominate Edward's government, and in the 1320s became the real ruler of England. He made himself astonishingly unpopular thanks to his almost pathological greed, despotism, taking of others' lands by illegal and quasi-legal methods, and his penchant for extortion and false imprisonment. One of the earliest signs that Despenser had risen high in Edward II's favour comes from a letter he wrote to the sheriff of his South Wales lordship of Glamorgan just after the siege of Berwick-upon-Tweed in September 1319. The letter makes it apparent that Despenser realised that he only had to ask the king for whatever he wanted, and his wish would be granted.

There is still much to see in Berwick-upon-Tweed. The castle Edward II would have known, originally built by King David I of Scotland (r. 1124–53) and rebuilt in the late 1290s by Edward's father, is now in ruins – sadly, much of what remained was torn down in the nineteenth century when the town's railway station was constructed – but a flight of steps and a large section of wall dating from Edward I's time still exist, and can be visited for free. It is possible to walk around the entire town of Berwick using the town walls and ramparts originally built in the Middle Ages. They were much modified in the sixteenth century and again in the seventeenth and eighteenth, but give an excellent idea of what the medieval fortified town looked like and how difficult the task of capturing Berwick was. Berwick (pronounced 'berrik') lies 20 miles north of the wonderful castle of Bamburgh, 30 miles north of Alnwick Castle, 30 miles south of the Scottish town of Dunbar (where Edward II fled after the battle of Bannockburn on 24 June 1314), 50 miles from Edinburgh, and 60 miles north of Newcastle-upon-Tyne. There is a railway station in the town, and it lies just off the A1, the road which connects London and Edinburgh. The famous Holy Island, or Lindisfarne, is just 12 miles south of Berwick.

Pickering Castle, Yorkshire: Partly Rebuilt by Edward

Pickering is a town which lies just outside the border of the North York Moors national park, 50 miles from Pontefract and 18 from Scarborough. A motte and bailey castle was built there by William the Conqueror in 1069/70 during his Harrying of the North – when the king marched his army into Yorkshire and did his utmost to destroy it – and was extended by his great-grandson Henry II. Edward II rebuilt much of the castle between 1323 and 1326.

King Henry III gave Pickering to his younger son Edmund of Lancaster, Edward II's uncle, in 1267, and it passed to Edmund's eldest son Thomas after Edmund's death in 1296. Thomas, earl of Lancaster and Leicester, was the worst enemy of his cousin Edward II for most of Edward's reign, and Edward finally had him executed outside his own castle of Pontefract on 22 March 1322. Thomas's heir, as he had no legitimate children, was his younger brother Henry. Edward II allowed Henry to have the earldom of Leicester in 1324 but not the earldom of Lancaster, and kept much of Henry's inheritance in his own hands, including Pickering.

Edward spent almost all of the period from March 1322 until October 1323 in the north of England, mostly in Yorkshire, and stayed at Pickering for two weeks in August 1323. He spent money rebuilding parts of the castle to improve its defences against possible future incursions by the Scots; the castle stands on the main route between the town of Helmsley, where there is another castle, and Scarborough, and was strategically important. Thomas of Lancaster had spent a great deal of money in the 1310s repairing and updating Pickering, and in May 1312 had sat here with an army while Piers Gaveston was besieged at Scarborough Castle a few miles away, as an extra line of defence against the royal favourite. After Pickering fell into Edward II's hands, he rebuilt the timber palisade around the outer bailey in stone, and this new stone wall had four towers which stand to this day: Rosamund's Tower, Mill Tower, Diate Hill Tower, and a gatehouse tower. Edward always took a keen interest in horses and in the 1320s kept a stud of more than fifty animals at Pickering, as well as two more at his royal manors of Woodstock in Oxfordshire and Burstwick in Yorkshire.

Pickering Castle is now looked after by English Heritage, and there is much to see and enjoy there. The church of St Peter and St Paul down the hill from the castle contains a number of magnificent wall paintings which date to around 1450, over a century after Edward II's time, but an absolute must for anyone interested in medieval history.

Church of Saint Thomas Becket (Saint Thomas the Martyr), Winchelsea, Sussex: Another Likeness of the King

In 1321/22, Edward II and his chamberlain Hugh Despenser the Younger made enemies of the Marcher lords, the men who held lordships in Wales and along the Welsh–English border. Disgruntled at Edward's increasing favouritism towards Despenser and the king's willingness to trample over ancient – albeit anachronistic – Marcher privileges to benefit his beloved, they formed themselves into a coalition and destroyed the English and Welsh lands of Despenser and his father Hugh the Elder in May 1321 during the so-called 'Despenser War'. The furious king soon took to calling his and Despenser's enemies the 'Contrariants'. After their orgy of destruction and vandalism across much of Wales and England in May 1321, the Contrariants travelled to Yorkshire to meet Thomas, earl of Lancaster, whom they considered their leader, then went south to London for parliament, sacking, robbing and destroying many manors on the way (not only Despenser manors). They sat menacingly with their armies around the walls of London to prevent Edward leaving, and forced him both to pardon them and all their followers for the appalling vandalism they had perpetrated across the country, and to exile the two Hugh Despensers permanently from their homeland. The Despensers' descendants were perpetually disinherited.

The two Despensers were given until 29 August 1321, the feast of the Beheading of St John the Baptist, to leave England and Wales forever. Hugh Despenser the Elder obediently did so, though where he went is not known; probably to one of Edward II's continental possessions such as Ponthieu or Gascony. Hugh the Younger, an altogether different character from his father, had no intention of doing what his enemies wished, and became a pirate in the English Channel. It is apparent that he did so with Edward's full knowledge and connivance, and he placed Despenser under the protection of the men of the Cinque Ports (Sandwich, Dover, Hastings, Hythe and Romney, plus the two Ancient Towns of Winchelsea and Rye) and thanked them in late November 1321 for looking after his beloved Despenser. Hugh Despenser the Younger may have taken part in an attack on Southampton on 30 September and 1 October 1321 in the company of some men from the Sussex port of Winchelsea, and he met Edward II secretly on at least a couple of occasions during his exile. Numerous contemporary chroniclers wrote about Despenser's piracy in the Channel; one called him a 'sea-monster'. Edward III belatedly paid compensation fifteen years later to several Italian merchants whose ships were attacked and robbed by his father's favourite.

Robert Batail of Winchelsea, a baron of the Cinque Ports and one of Edward II's admirals, may have been one of Hugh Despenser's pirate associates; it was he who carried out the 1321 attack on Southampton. Other fellow pirates may have included members of the Alard family, a famous sailing dynasty from Winchelsea. Edward pardoned Stephen and Robert Alard for piracy on 6 May 1322, though they continued their activities that year and into 1323 in the company of Robert Batail, and the port of Winchelsea was notorious for piracy in the thirteenth and early fourteenth centuries. Edward kept in close touch with Stephen Alard, admiral of the western fleet and of the Cinque Ports, in the 1320s.

A tomb believed to be Stephen Alard's in St Thomas Becket's Church in Winchelsea features a monument with stone heads believed to represent Edward II and his queen Isabella of France. The image of Edward in the church resembles other extant depictions of him, such as the effigy on his tomb in Gloucester Cathedral and a stone corbel inside the great hall of Caerphilly Castle in South Wales. Edward is always shown with a bushy beard and with long wavy or curly hair falling either side of his face, usually held in place with a crown or coronet. Edward's hair may have been fair, and he probably stood at least 6ft tall; his father, Edward I's, embalmed remains in Westminster Abbey were measured in 1774 and he was found to have stood 6ft 2in inches. Edward III's life-size death effigy measured 5ft 10½in. Contemporary chroniclers all describe Edward II in the same way: tall, handsome and enormously strong. The *Vita Edwardi Secundi* called him 'tall and strong, a fine figure of a handsome man', the *Scalacronica* declared that 'physically he was one of the strongest men in his realm', the *Anonimalle* said that he was 'a handsome man, strong of body and limb', and the *Gesta Edwardi de Carnarvon* called him 'elegant, of outstanding strength'. Other descriptions paint the same picture, and Edward II was as far removed from the depiction of him as a weak, feeble court fop in the Hollywood film *Braveheart* as any man possibly could be.

Some of the Alard tombs are thought to have been moved from the church in Old Winchelsea on Romney Marsh after the port was washed away during a terrible storm in February 1287 (when the future Edward II was not quite 3 years old). The church of St Thomas Becket or St Thomas the Martyr was begun around 1290, 120 years after Becket's murder in Canterbury Cathedral. Edward met Hugh Despenser the Younger secretly at least once during Despenser's exile from England in late 1321 and early 1322, probably in Winchelsea or rather, in a boat off the coast there. Although the port does not feature on his known itinerary at that time, in March 1322 the king thanked the barons of Winchelsea for giving him advice 'when the king was lately on the sea' with them, and for supporting him and Despenser in their struggle against the Contrariants, in which they would soon emerge victorious.

Leeds Castle, Kent: Besieged by Edward

Leeds is a fairy-tale castle, built on two islands in the middle of a lake; its official website calls it 'the loveliest castle in the world', and it is hard to disagree. It belonged to Edward II's mother Leonor of Castile, the Spanish queen of England, who bought it in 1278, and it passed to Edward as her only surviving son and heir. Edward's father probably rebuilt much of the castle and made it the glorious wonder it is today. Much less happily, Edward II himself besieged Leeds in October 1321, hanged thirteen members of the garrison, and used his attack on the castle as a ploy to begin a campaign against his baronial enemies and to bring his friends the two Hugh Despensers back to England from exile.

In August 1321, Edward II was forced by the Marcher lords to consent to the perpetual exile and disinheritance of his beloved chamberlain Hugh Despenser the Younger and Despenser's father, Hugh the Elder. The king had no intention of allowing the Despensers to remain outside England for very long or to let their foes win, and told his ally the bishop of Rochester that he would deal with the Marcher lords in such a way that 'the whole world would hear of it and tremble'. Despenser the Younger returned to England at least once, and probably twice, to meet the king and to plot their next moves; many of their schemes to bring down their Marcher enemies revolved around Leeds Castle in Kent.

Edward's stepmother Marguerite of France, second wife of Edward I and the dowager queen of England, held Leeds from 1307 until 1318. After her death in February 1318, Edward II did not give Leeds to his wife Isabella, but to Bartholomew, Lord Badlesmere, a baron of Kent and an influential politician in England between 1317 and 1321. Badlesmere was elected steward of the king's household in 1318 at the same time that Hugh Despenser the Younger was elected its chamberlain, and for a few years Badlesmere and Despenser were close allies; they were jointly involved in some deeply shady business in 1319 or 1320 when they illegally took a man out of prison in Colchester and forced him to sign over his manor in Essex to Badlesmere. Until late June 1321, Bartholomew Badlesmere was still a close ally of Edward II and Despenser, but switched sides when the king sent him to Yorkshire to spy on a meeting between Thomas, earl of Lancaster, and his Marcher allies. Badlesmere had close relations with two of the chief Marcher lords: Roger, Lord Clifford, was his wife's nephew, and Roger Mortimer, lord of Wigmore's son and heir

Edmund was married to Badlesmere's daughter Elizabeth. His decision to defect to the Marchers was to result in his appalling death a few months later.

Bartholomew Badlesmere was geographically isolated in the county of Kent from his new allies, whereas Edward II's supporters, such as his half-brother Edmund of Woodstock (made earl of Kent in July 1321), John de Warenne, earl of Surrey and Sussex, Edmund Fitzalan, earl of Arundel, and Aymer de Valence, earl of Pembroke, were strong in that part of the country. Badlesmere, in his seat at Leeds Castle, therefore was a useful target for Edward and Despenser to begin their campaign against the Marchers. Edward deliberately sent his queen Isabella of France to Leeds Castle in early October 1321, and to demand entry (the queen had supposedly been on pilgrimage to Canterbury as a plausible excuse for being in Kent, but her return journey from there to London would not have taken her anywhere near Leeds Castle). Badlesmere, well aware of how furious Edward was with him for switching sides, had put all his Kent castles in a state of defence, and although he was not present at Leeds, his wife Margaret was there and fell into the king's trap by refusing to allow the queen entry.

The king and queen had the right to enter any home or castle in England and Wales that they wished, and Lady Badlesmere's refusal to permit Isabella to enter Leeds Castle was therefore a gross insult to the royal couple. Edward II feigned outrage at the Badlesmeres' behaviour, though he must have been delighted that all had gone to plan, and on 16 October 1321 announced his decision to besiege Leeds. Given the family connections between Bartholomew Badlesmere and the Marcher lords, if Edward struck at Badlesmere, they would probably feel honour-bound to come to his aid and would thus be in armed rebellion against the king which would give Edward an excuse to attack them. Edward also knew that his first cousin and greatest enemy, Thomas, earl of Lancaster, loathed Badlesmere, and gambled that Lancaster would therefore not come to the baron's aid. In this way, the king could divide and conquer his enemies.

Edward II's army mustered at Leeds on 23 October, and the king himself arrived there on the 26th; apparently bored, he ordered his hunting-dogs brought to him. As he had predicted, Badlesmere begged his new allies to help him, which put the Marchers in a very awkward position as they neither wished to take up arms against their king, nor to be seen to condone the insult Badlesmere's wife had recently offered Queen Isabella. The earl of Lancaster also played into Edward's hands; he sent the Marchers a letter, ordering them not to aid the detested Badlesmere. Unwilling, however, to abandon him entirely, they moved nearer to him and took their forces to Kingston-upon-Thames, and this gave Edward the excuse he needed to go after them. He began preparing a campaign to the west of England, the Marcher lords' territory, in November 1321.

As for Leeds Castle, the garrison surrendered to Edward on 31 October 1321, only five days after he had arrived there, and the vindictive king had thirteen of the men hanged. Executing members of a castle garrison for holding out against the king was not unprecedented – King Stephen hanged almost a hundred of the defenders of Shrewsbury Castle in 1138 – but by 1321, it had not been done within living memory. And as for the unfortunate Bartholomew, Lord Badlesmere, Edward II sent out safe-conducts for some of the Marchers to come to him in person and talk in late 1321 and early 1322, but pointedly excluded Badlesmere by name; the king never forgot or forgave a betrayal. After the Marcher lords lost the battle of Boroughbridge to a royalist army in March 1322 (see below), Edward's Scottish friend Donald of Mar captured Badlesmere at his nephew the bishop of Lincoln's manor of Stow Park in Lincolnshire where he had been hiding, and took him the long way south to Kent. On 14 April 1322, Badlesmere was dragged by horses to the crossroads at Blean and there suffered the traitor's death by hanging, drawing and quartering. His head was stuck on the gate leading into the city of Canterbury, 22 miles from Leeds Castle, as a warning to those who would betray the king. Fourteenth-century justice was swift, harsh and brutal.

After Edward II's turbulent reign and his execution of Leeds Castle's garrison in 1321, the castle's story became far quieter and more peaceful, and it passed into the ownership of Edward's wife Isabella of France until her death in 1358. Edward II and Isabella's great-grandson Richard II gave Leeds to his beloved queen Anne of Bohemia (1366–94) shortly after their wedding in 1382, and in the early fifteenth century it belonged to Juana of Navarre (c. 1370–1437), second wife of Richard II's first cousin and usurper Henry IV, and afterwards to Katherine de Valois (1401–37), the French wife of Henry V and mother of Henry VI. Katherine de Valois's great-grandson Henry VIII made major improvements to Leeds between 1517 and 1523, and he and his first queen, Katherine of Aragon, often stayed there.

As well as the stunning castle itself, the Leeds site also includes a maze, extensive gardens, two huge adventure playgrounds for children called the 'knights' realm' and 'squires' court', punting on the moat, a birds of prey centre with falconry displays, woodland, parkland and lakes. It can be hired for weddings, conferences and other events. Leeds Castle is 5 miles from Maidstone, and just an hour from central London. It can easily be reached by car from the M20 motorway, or by bus or train; the nearest railway station is Bearsted, and there is a regular shuttle service from there to the castle.

Boroughbridge, Yorkshire: Victory for Edward's Army

It is telling that the only real military victory of Edward II's reign was a battle at which he was not personally present. Edward set off to the west of England in late 1321 to face the Marcher lords who had forced the exile of Hugh Despenser and his father. Two of the king's main enemies were men he had once been remarkably close to, and had married two of his nieces in 1317: Sir Hugh Audley and Sir Roger Damory. Hugh Despenser had ousted them from Edward's side and his favour, and they joined the Marcher rebellion against Despenser and, by extension, the king. The Marchers refused to meet Edward in battle in late 1321 and early 1322, and fled from him; some of them, including Lord Berkeley of Berkeley Castle in Gloucestershire and Roger Mortimer, lord of Wigmore in Herefordshire, submitted to Edward at Shrewsbury in January and February 1322 and were imprisoned. The others, including Bartholomew Badlesmere, fled towards Yorkshire to their last hope; the king's cousin and greatest enemy, Thomas of Lancaster, earl of Lancaster and Leicester, the richest man in the country and the only one who could mount any kind of serious resistance to Edward.

The 'Contrariants' and Thomas of Lancaster committed treason by sending letters to Robert Bruce, king of Scotland, and asking him to send men to help them fight against their own king. The letters, in which Thomas of Lancaster referred to himself by the conceited pseudonym 'King Arthur', were discovered by agents of the archbishop of York, and the king ordered all his sheriffs to make their contents public. Edward travelled from Shropshire towards Yorkshire in February and

March 1322, capturing his former beloved companion and nephew-in-law Roger Damory at Burton-on-Trent, Staffordshire, on the way. Damory died of wounds sustained fighting against the royal army, shortly after the king had respited the death sentence imposed on him; his wife Elizabeth de Burgh, née de Clare, the king's niece, had now been widowed for the third time at the age of only 26 and outlived Damory by almost forty years. (A few years later, the wealthy Elizabeth founded Clare College at Cambridge.) Damory's allies joined Thomas of Lancaster at his stronghold of Pontefract in Yorkshire, and after much debate they decided to flee to Thomas's recently built castle of Dunstanburgh, on the coast of Northumberland.

The Contrariants had only managed to ride 30 miles from Pontefract to the town of Boroughbridge, where the Great North Road met the River Ure, when they found Andrew Harclay, Sheriff of Yorkshire, waiting for them. They were forced into battle in Boroughbridge on 16 March. The town had, perhaps ironically, once belonged to Piers Gaveston, earl of Cornwall. The royalist army led by the loyal Andrew Harclay took up the same formations called schiltrons (men standing close together holding long pikes facing outwards as defensive shield walls) which had been used to great effect against Edward II and his cavalry at Bannockburn, guarding the narrow bridge over the Ure, and defeated the Contrariants. Edward's own brother-in-law Humphrey de Bohun, earl of Hereford (b. c. 1276), fighting for the Contrariants, died horribly, with a lance thrust up his back passage by a Welsh soldier hiding under the bridge. The earl of Lancaster asked for an overnight truce, during which many of the Contrariants' soldiers deserted and fled, and surrendered to Andrew Harclay the following day. It was a great victory for the royalists, the only real military victory of Edward II's reign, and he personally did not take part.

A contemporary chronicler gives an account of how the Contrariant knights and noblemen who had fought at Boroughbridge tried to escape after their defeat: 'Some left their horses and putting off their armour looked round for ancient worn-out garments, and took to the road as beggars. But their caution was of no avail, for not a single well-known man among them all escaped.' Some men tried to flee the country or to hide by donning religious habits. Edward sent out members of his household both to arrest the fleeing Contrariants and to seize the horses and possessions they had abandoned in their flight, and local inhabitants joined in the hunt. Eleven men were captured 35 miles away at Selby the day after the battle, and their goods were sent to the king. They included a pair of silk garters adorned with silver and red enamel with a cross bar of silver, a 'great silver chain', twelve buttons of green glass adorned with silver gilt, eight of silver wire and five of white silver, seven pearls the size of peas, a silk purse, a book worth ten shillings, eight horses, six silver dishes, two 'worn swords' and an old dagger. One of the noblemen captured after the battle of Boroughbridge was Edward II's nephew-in-law Sir Hugh Audley, who would spend the remainder of Edward's reign in prison; his wife Margaret, née de Clare, the king's niece and Piers Gaveston's widow, spent more than four-and-a-half years incarcerated at Sempringham Priory in Lincolnshire and was finally released in December 1326 after the downfall of her uncle the king and her brother-in-law, Hugh Despenser the Younger. Edward II proved to be remarkably vindictive in the aftermath of his army's victory at Boroughbridge, and within four years had managed to alienate his queen, his half-brothers, his cousins Henry of Lancaster and John of Brittany, most of his bishops, and just about everybody else. With his enemies either dead or in prison or exile, and wealthy as a result of the forfeitures of the Marcher lords, he had the chance to salvage his failed reign in and after 1322; but he failed to take it.

The Yorkshire town of Boroughbridge is 10 miles from Harrogate, 17 miles from York and 7 miles from Knaresborough Castle, detailed elsewhere. Just off the A1 road, it can easily be reached by car.

Pontefract Castle, Yorkshire: Edward Executes his Cousin

Pontefract was one of the greatest castles in the country until the aftermath of the Civil War in the 1640s. It was a royalist stronghold during the war and was besieged several times by parliamentary forces, and in and after 1649, Oliver Cromwell took the decision to 'slight', i.e. knock down, the castle. Today only a few ruins still exist, though an extant seventeenth-century painting gives some idea of its vastness and splendour. The castle was built around 1070 by Ilbert de Lacy, an ally of William the Conqueror, and it passed down the de Lacy family for almost two-and-a-half centuries. Henry de Lacy, earl of Lincoln, died in February 1311 at the age of about 60, and Pontefract Castle and his other numerous land and castles passed to his only surviving child Alice (b. 1281) and her husband Thomas (b. 1277/78), earl of Lancaster and Leicester. Thomas was by far the most royal and highly born of the English earls of Edward II's reign, and thanks to the earldoms he inherited from his father and from his parents-in-law, he was the richest man in the country after his cousin the king, with an annual income of about £11,000 (at a time when most people in England earned between one and three pence per day). Despite his vast wealth Thomas was notoriously extravagant and spent about 20 per cent more than he earned, and had to borrow money from the people of his town of Leicester on several occasions.

Thomas began Edward II's reign in 1307 as a staunch ally and supporter of his cousin, and the two men had also been close before Edward's accession to the throne; in 1305 Edward sent Thomas a letter stating that he understood Thomas could not attend him because he was too ill to travel, and that he would visit Thomas instead 'to see and to comfort you'. However, something went badly wrong between the two royal cousins in about late 1308; perhaps they quarrelled and were too stubborn to make up afterwards, but whatever happened, Thomas began to move into a position of opposition to Edward, and the men came to loathe each other. Thomas refused to come into the king's presence without a safe-conduct, and he was the chief mover in the murder, or execution, of Piers Gaveston in Warwickshire on 19 June 1312. Various chroniclers comment on the 'hatred which endured forever' between the cousins as a result, and Thomas must have known that killing Gaveston was the one thing Edward would never be able to forgive.

After Thomas of Lancaster's father-in-law, Henry de Lacy, died in February 1311, Pontefract became Thomas's favourite residence (Thomas's wife Alice, meanwhile, seems to have spent more time at Bolingbroke Castle in Lincolnshire, which she had also inherited from her father Henry, and left her husband and their unhappy childless marriage in 1317). By 1316, Thomas and Edward II had taken to ostentatiously marching around the country with armed men deliberately avoiding each other, and when they did meet on one occasion, in York in August 1316, they had a furious quarrel. The king passed through Pontefract in the autumn of 1317 on his way from York to London, and astonishingly, the earl of Lancaster led his men out onto the battlements of his castle to jeer at the king and his retinue as they rode past. Edward came very close to ordering an attack on Pontefract Castle, understandably furious, but fortunately was talked out of it by his and Lancaster's cousin the earl of

Pembroke; such an act would have led to civil war. The king never forgot or forgave, however, and raised Thomas's ill-mannered jeering as one of the many charges against his cousin at the earl's trial inside Pontefract Castle a few years later.

The two cousins made a mutual treaty of friendship in August 1318 after long and strenuous efforts by a number of the English earls, bishops and barons to reconcile them, and both men did make an effort to get on for the next year or so; Thomas witnessed almost forty of Edward's charters in 1318 and 1319 and was very often at court, and took part in Edward's unsuccessful siege of the port of Berwick-upon-Tweed in September 1319. It was here, however, that things went badly wrong again. Thomas was accused, probably unfairly, of conspiring with Robert Bruce and his men to allow them to capture his niece Queen Isabella, and left the port after another quarrel with Edward, whereupon the king declared ominously that after the siege was over, he would 'turn [his] hands to other matters', as he had 'not forgotten the wrong that was done to my brother Piers'. The execution of Piers Gaveston (whom Edward II, unable to acknowledge publicly as his lover, generally referred to as his 'brother') and Thomas's role in it still preyed on Edward's mind more than seven years later.

The Marcher lords or 'Contrariants' who rebelled against Edward II and Hugh Despenser the Younger in 1321/22 saw Thomas as their leader, and met him in Yorkshire in June 1321, a few weeks before they attended parliament in London and demanded the exile of the two Hugh Despensers. Lancaster, who by now spent almost all of his time at his castle in Pontefract – he may have suffered from some kind of long-term disease or disability and seems often to have been ill – played no active role in the destruction of Despenser and his father's lands across South Wales and England, nor in the early months of the Contrariant resistance to the king in late 1321 and early 1322. In early March 1322, the remaining Contrariants fled to Pontefract to join the earl of Lancaster, their only hope of protection. When their letters to Scotland asking its king Robert Bruce to send men to help them fight against Edward II were discovered, this was clearly treason, and almost a decade after Piers Gaveston's murder Edward finally had the excuse he needed to have his cousin executed.

After the earl of Lancaster and his army's defeat at the battle of Boroughbridge on 16 March 1322, Lancaster was taken to the city of York and from there via water to Pontefract Castle, whose constable immediately surrendered to Edward when the king arrived there on 19 March. Edward waited at Pontefract for his cousin. With him were Hugh Despenser the Younger and his father Hugh the Elder, who had returned to England in or before early March 1322, barely six months after their sentence of perpetual exile from England in late August 1321. Most of the English earls alive in 1322 were also there: the king's half-brothers Norfolk and Kent, his nephew-in-law Surrey and Surrey's brother-in-law Arundel, and Edward's cousin the earl of Pembroke. The Scottish earls of Atholl and Angus were also present, supporting the king, and the only English earls not there were Lancaster himself; Hereford – who had been killed at the battle of Boroughbridge; Oxford, who was completely insignificant and played no role at all in Edward II's reign; and Edward's son and the heir to the throne, Edward of Windsor, earl of Chester, who was only 9 years old.

Thomas, earl of Lancaster, was forced to put on garments of the striped cloth which the squires of his household wore, an intentional humiliation of a man of high birth and rank. On the way from Boroughbridge to York, a crowd of people threw snowballs at him, called him a traitor, and shouted: 'Now shall you have the reward that long time you have deserved!' According to a rumour reported by the contemporary writer of the *Vita Edwardi Secundi* (Life of Edward II), the earl had built a tower in which to hold the king captive for the rest of his life once he defeated him, but Lancaster was imprisoned there instead. A triumphant Hugh Despenser the Younger took the opportunity to hurl 'malicious and contemptuous words' into Lancaster's face on his arrival at Pontefract. Lancaster was put on trial in the great hall of his own castle, where the justice Robert Malberthorpe, the king, the two Hugh Despensers, and the earls of Kent, Pembroke, Richmond, Surrey, Arundel, Angus and Atholl sat in judgement on him. The result was a foregone conclusion, and Lancaster was not allowed to speak in his own defence as his crimes were deemed 'notorious', known to everybody. He exclaimed: 'This is a powerful court, and great in authority, where no answer is heard nor any excuse admitted', but given that he himself had executed Piers Gaveston without a trial in June 1312 he hardly had grounds for complaint.

Lancaster's judges sentenced him to death by hanging, drawing and quartering, though Edward commuted the sentence to mere beheading, respiting the hanging and drawing either out of love for Queen Isabella according to one chronicler, or out of respect for Lancaster's royal blood according to two others. Edward arranged Lancaster's execution as a parody of Gaveston's death, and the parallels between the deaths of Gaveston and Lancaster did not go unnoticed by contemporaries. The earl could easily have been beheaded in the castle bailey, but Edward had him taken outside to a small hill, as Gaveston had been killed on Blacklow Hill. Lancaster was forced to ride a 'worthless mule' and 'an old chaplet, rent and torn' was set on his head (presumably he still wore the striped cloth of his household squires). A crowd of spectators again threw snowballs at him; the winter of 1321/22 was a long and cold one, and snow lay on the ground for most of the first three months of 1322. At the king's order, the great earl was made to kneel facing Scotland in a pointed reminder of his treason, and the executioner took two or three strokes of the axe to remove his head. Thomas, earl of Lancaster, Leicester, Lincoln and Salisbury, was buried in the church of Pontefract Priory, and decades later his nephew and heir Henry of Grosmont, first duke of Lancaster (c. 1310–61) had a chapel built on the site where he died. Oddly enough, Thomas of Lancaster gained a reputation for sanctity and miracles, and until the Reformation in the sixteenth century was an unofficial Yorkshire saint; items of his clothing were preserved at Pontefract and for more than 200 years were deemed to aid women in childbirth. Thomas's great-nephew, Edward III, wrote to the pope and cardinals on several occasions asking them to canonise Thomas as a saint, though this was more a political act and a sign that Thomas's brother and nephew were high in the king's favour rather than an indication that Edward III really believed that Thomas was saintly.

The execution of the wealthy and royal earl of Lancaster shocked the country. Thomas was, not counting Piers Gaveston in 1312 (as it is not clear whether Gaveston was legally earl of Cornwall when he died), the first English earl to be executed since William the Conqueror had earl Waltheof beheaded in 1076. Everyone, including surely Thomas himself, believed that his royal blood would save him from execution. Edward II, however, had never forgiven him for Gaveston's death, and although it took him ten years, he finally managed to manoeuvre Thomas into a position where he had a reason to execute him and to take revenge for Gaveston.

Pontefract Castle has another strong, and unhappy, connection to the medieval English royal family. Edward II's great-grandson Richard II died there on or about 14 February 1400. He had been forced to abdicate his throne the previous September to his first cousin Henry, third duke of Lancaster, great-great-nephew and heir of Thomas of Lancaster, who became Henry IV and was crowned king of England at Westminster Abbey on 13 October 1399. The new king sent his cousin, now merely Sir Richard of Bordeaux, to imprisonment at Pontefract Castle, both because it was remote from London and from possible rescue attempts, and also because Edward II, the great-grandfather venerated by Richard II, had had Thomas of Lancaster executed there. Edward II won his battle against a wealthy and troublesome Lancastrian first cousin, at least for a while (Thomas's brother and heir Henry played an important role in his downfall and deposition in 1326/27); Richard II lost his, and paid the ultimate price for it.

The town of Pontefract lies in West Yorkshire, between Leeds and Doncaster. A few ruins of its once great castle still remain, and a major conservation project has taken place there in recent years to preserve what is left. The ruins are open all year round and are free to visit. There are tours of the extant dungeons on Thursdays, Saturdays and Sundays, and more are scheduled during school holidays. Pontefract Castle has a full schedule of events around the year, including a 'siege weekend', St George's Day celebrations, Proms in the Castle and an Easter Trail. There is a visitor centre, café and gift shop.

An easy 4-mile drive from Pontefract lies the village of Brotherton, where Edward II's half-brother Thomas of Brotherton, earl of Norfolk and Earl Marshal of England, was born on 1 June 1300. Thomas was the elder of Edward I's two sons with his second wife Marguerite of France (1278/9–1318), and made a rather obscure marriage c. 1321 to Alice Hales, daughter of the coroner of Norfolk. His heir was his eldest child Margaret (c. 1322–99), the first Englishwoman to be made a duchess in her own right in 1397, and Edward I's last surviving grandchild. Margaret of Norfolk was imprisoned in Somerton Castle, Lincolnshire, by her cousin Edward III in 1354, as detailed elsewhere in this volume. Thomas of Brotherton, via his daughter Margaret and Margaret's daughter Elizabeth Mowbray, née Segrave, was the ancestor of the fifteenth-century Mowbray dukes of Norfolk and of their successors the Howards, and was thus the ancestor of two of Henry VIII's wives, Anne Boleyn and Katherine Howard.

The village of East Cowick, 15 miles east of Pontefract, was a royal manor where Edward II spent much time during his long sojourn in

Yorkshire from March 1322, after Thomas of Lancaster's execution, until March 1323, and then again in May, June and August 1323. His great-niece Margaret Despenser, fourth daughter of Hugh Despenser the Younger and Edward's eldest niece Eleanor, née de Clare, was born at Cowick at the beginning of August 1323, and the king gave a generous gift of £100 to Eleanor for 'the expenses of her childbed'. Hugh Despenser the Younger's nemesis, Roger Mortimer of Wigmore, escaped from the Tower of London on 1 August 1323, probably the day that Despenser's daughter was born.

Clifford's Tower, York: Edward Executes Two Noblemen

As well as Thomas, earl of Lancaster, Edward II had around twenty or so Contrariants, all of them noblemen and knights, executed in March and April 1322, and dozens more were imprisoned. The Contrariants had committed serious crimes such as homicide, assault, false imprisonment, plunder, vandalism, extortion and theft (even from churches) between May 1321 and March 1322. Two of the executed Contrariants were Roger, Lord Clifford, and John, Lord Mowbray, both hanged in chains in York on 23 March 1322 at a fortification whose name commemorates Lord Clifford to this day.

Roger, Lord Clifford, was the son and heir of Robert, Lord Clifford, who was killed fighting for Edward II at Bannockburn in June 1314 and who, as a handsome 26-year-old in 1300, had proved remarkably popular with the English heralds who wrote the poem about the siege of Caerlaverock Castle (see above). The Cliffords were an old noble family, and Henry II's famous mistress Rosamund Clifford (d. 1176) was one of them. Until Edward II's reign the family had owned most of their lands in the Marches, the English–Welsh borderlands, but Robert (1274–1314) inherited territories in Cumberland, Westmorland and Yorkshire from his mother Isabel Vipont (d. 1292), and Edward II granted him the Yorkshire castle and manor of Skipton in 1310. The Cliffords remained prominent at Skipton for centuries; Robert's descendant Lady Anne Clifford (1590–1676), countess of Dorset and Pembroke and High Sheriff of Westmorland, was born at Skipton Castle, and to this day is a famous figure in the north of England.

Robert Clifford's eldest son Roger, born in 1299 or 1300, was about 22 at the time of his execution and never married or had children, and therefore his heir was his younger brother Robert, who was only 16 at the time of the Contrariant rebellion and took no part in it. Roger Clifford was hanged at Clifford's Tower in York alongside his Contrariant ally John, Lord Mowbray (b. 1286), whose Mowbray descendants became dukes of Norfolk at the end of the fourteenth century. John Mowbray's wife Aline, née Braose, and their son John, born in November 1310, were imprisoned for a while in the Tower of London by Edward II in early 1322, despite John's youth. In April 1326, though he was still only 15, the younger John demonstrated his anger with the king who had executed his father and imprisoned him and his mother by besieging and capturing the royal castle of Tickhill in Yorkshire, whose custodian, William Aune, was a friend of Edward II.

Clifford's Tower is the inner keep and all that now remains of York Castle. The castle was originally built just after the Norman Conquest of 1066, and tragically, 150 Jews were killed there in March 1190, or committed suicide to avoid falling into the hands of the mob besieging them, during a wave of anti-Jewish feeling and pogroms sweeping through England. Edward II's grandfather Henry III rebuilt the Tower in stone in the middle of the thirteenth century, though work was not completed until early in Edward II's lifetime in the 1290s. Henry III would have seen the work progressing when his daughter Margaret married King Alexander III of Scotland in York at Christmas 1251; she was 11 and he 10, and their granddaughter Margaret 'the Maid' of Norway was betrothed to Edward of Caernarfon in 1289 when she was 6 and he 5. Edward II himself spent much time in York throughout his reign, and often stayed at the friary of the Franciscans just outside the city walls.

Clifford's Tower stands in the centre of York, at the top of a steep earth mound, and provides excellent views over the city. It is a quatrefoil design and resembles a four-leafed clover; it stands 50ft high and is about 200ft in diameter. The name 'Clifford's Tower' was only recorded in 1596, though almost certainly it was named after Roger Clifford. The king finally gave permission in April 1324 for the remains of all the twenty or so executed Contrariants to be taken down and buried; Roger Clifford's and John Mowbray's bodies had hung on the walls of Clifford's Tower for two years. Edward II must have seen them when he spent Christmas 1322 in the city of York.

Rievaulx Abbey and the Battlefield of Old Byland, Yorkshire: Edward is Almost Captured

In mid-August 1322, some months after his victory over the Contrariants, Edward led a military campaign to Scotland which proved as much of an unsuccessful, expensive failure as all his others, and also proved to be his last. Having achieved nothing at all, the king returned to England in September, and in mid-October 1322 stayed at Rievaulx Abbey in Yorkshire. Robert Bruce, king of Scotland, launched a counter-invasion of England at the end of September 1322, and his forces reached as far south as Chorley in Lancashire, on the western side of England, and within 25 miles of York on the eastern side. Unbeknownst to Edward, a large Scottish force marched rapidly towards him in mid-October. Edward II hastily, and belatedly, scrambled a force to meet Robert and his army at Blackhow Moor, now called Sutton Bank and Roulston Scar, several miles from Rievaulx Abbey and some miles from the village of Old Byland, and between the towns of Thirsk and Helmsley.

The Battle of Byland, named after the nearest village, Old Byland, was fought on 14 October 1322 between English and Scottish forces, though Edward II did not personally take part. The leader of the English force was Edward's first cousin John of Brittany, earl of Richmond, son of Edward I's sister Beatrice (1242–75) and the uncle of the reigning duke of Brittany, John III. Richmond was born c. 1266 so was 56 years old in 1322, about eighteen years Edward II's senior, and had never shown much in the way of abilities or leadership. He lost the battle of Byland and was taken prisoner, and Edward had to pay an enormous ransom for him (which, considering that Richmond joined Queen Isabella after she rebelled against Edward in 1325/26, he can hardly have deemed worth it). One man who might have fought on the English side was none other than Robert Bruce's nephew Donald, earl of Mar, who had been taken prisoner by Edward I as a child in 1306 and was incarcerated at Bristol Castle. Donald soon became, however, a staunch ally of Edward II and joined his household, and declined to return to his homeland when Edward had to free all the Scottish hostages in England after the battle of Bannockburn in 1314. He remained with Edward until the king's downfall in late 1326.

The earl of Richmond lost the battle and his own freedom, but his sacrifice gave Edward II the time he needed to escape. To avoid capture by Robert's forces, Edward and his retinue had to gallop the 50 miles to the town of Bridlington on the coast (the city of York, 25 miles south of Rievaulx, was much closer, but the way there led through what are now called the Howardian Hills and the journey to Bridlington was much easier). With him were his chamberlain Hugh Despenser the Younger, his half-brother Edmund of Woodstock, earl of Kent, and his former household steward Sir John Cromwell. It was the second time the king of England had had to flee from a Scottish force, and although his flight to avoid capture and ransom after the battle of Bannockburn in June 1314 made perfect sense, his flight in October 1322 was over 100 miles within the borders of his own kingdom and was a deep humiliation both for Edward himself and for his subjects. The Lanercost chronicler in the far north-west of England, writing a couple of decades later, called Edward II 'ever chicken-hearted and luckless in war' (the second part is certainly true, but the first seems unduly harsh and judgemental; Edward was no general, but he was certainly no coward either). The Bridlington chronicler, writing at the priory where Edward stayed after fleeing from Rievaulx, asked rhetorically: 'What worse fate could befall the English than to behold their king fleeing from place to place in the face of the Scots?'

Edward II left Rievaulx in such a hurry that he was forced to abandon his personal belongings, and the appreciative Scots kept them as they had also done with his baggage train after Bannockburn. Edward had lost his great seal after Bannockburn, and at Rievaulx lost his privy seal, though Robert, as he had done eight years previously, courteously sent it back to him. Edward remained in Yorkshire for a few weeks after his near-capture, and in late November 1322 the unconventional king stood by a river near Doncaster and watched a group of men fishing; given that he thoroughly enjoyed fishing, he may even have joined in. Edward spent Christmas 1322 in York, and a later chronicler commented that his heart was 'savagely tormented'. On Christmas Day the king enjoyed a feast of porpoise, sturgeon, swans, peacocks, herons, pigeons, venison and wild boar, and on 26 December paid two women for singing in his garden at the Franciscan friary in York. The king may have been 'savagely tormented', but he still ate and lived well.

Rievaulx Abbey lies in a deep valley three miles from the town of Helmsley, and belonged to the austere Cistercian order. It was founded in 1132, and its name is the French version of 'Ryevale'; it is pronounced 'ree-voh'. The abbey was closed down in 1538 during the Dissolution of the Monasteries, but much still remains, including the gorgeous abbey church, the cloisters, the infirmary complex and the refectory (though they are all now open to the elements). The abbey church was built in the 1140s and heightened in the 1220s, a rebuilding visible to this day in the lighter stone and larger windows of the higher storeys. Items excavated at Rievaulx, now on display there, include objects which once belonged to Edward II and which were left behind in his desperate haste to flee from the Scottish force in October 1322.

Romantic artists of the eighteenth and nineteenth centuries depicted Rievaulx's glorious ruins, and in the mid-eighteenth century Rievaulx Terrace was built on the hill above the ruins: a grass-covered terrace with two Palladian temples as follies. The village of Old Byland, less than 3 miles from the abbey, has an ancient Grade I Listed church, All Saints, dating from the early Norman era with features dating back to Saxon times; if Edward II ever saw the church when he visited the area, he would certainly still recognise it today. Helmsley Castle, 3 miles from Rievaulx, was owned by one of the sons-in-law of Bartholomew, Lord Badlesmere, a Contrariant whom Edward executed near Canterbury in April 1322, six months before his flight from Rievaulx, and there are still extensive remains there. Rievaulx stands in a deep valley 30 miles north of York, and is difficult to reach by public transport, with the nearest railway station at Thirsk 11 miles away, and the nearest bus stop in Helmsley.

Pickering Castle is 15 miles from Rievaulx, and Boroughbridge, where Edward II's army defeated the Contrariants in March 1322, is 23 miles. The escarpment where the battle of Byland was fought on 14 October 1322, then called Blackhow Moor, is now called Sutton Bank and Roulston Scar, and the A170 road between Thirsk and Helmsley winds up the remarkably steep hill where a Scottish force defeated the king of England's army and almost captured the king himself.

Ten miles from Rievaulx stands Newburgh Priory, an Augustinian house founded in 1145, where Edward II stayed from 23 October until 8 November 1316. While he was there, he listened to the performance of a violist sent to him by his second cousin Philip (1278–1332), king of Albania, Prince of Achaea (in Greece) and Taranto (in Italy), despot of Epirus (in Greece and Albania) and titular emperor of Constantinople, an interesting example of how Edward and his relatives on the far side of Europe kept in touch. After Newburgh was closed down in 1538 during the Dissolution of the Monasteries, it was turned into a stately home which is now open to the public several days of the week from April to June, and has a water garden, walled garden and woodland. It can be hired for weddings.

Tynemouth Priory and Castle, North Tyneside: Burial Site of Edward's Illegitimate Son

The priory at Tynemouth dates back to the early seventh century, when it was founded probably by Edwin, king of Northumbria, who converted to Christianity in 627 and was later venerated as a saint. It was sacked by the Danes in 800 and again in 870, and for 200 years the priory lay forgotten; it was re-founded in about 1090 by the earl of Northumbria, Robert Mowbray, a Norman who had come to England with William the Conqueror. Tynemouth Priory was already ancient in Edward II's time, and it features three times in his story. First, he, Queen Isabella and Piers Gaveston stayed here in April and early May 1312, and Gaveston was almost captured by Edward's cousin and enemy Thomas of Lancaster. Second, Isabella was here again in October 1322 when she came close to capture by the Scottish force who had recently defeated her husband's forces at the battle of Old Byland, and she accused Edward's chamberlain Hugh Despenser the Younger of abandoning her there deliberately. Third, Edward II's illegitimate son Adam was buried at Tynemouth Priory on 30 September 1322, still in his teens at most or perhaps as young as 12 years old.

After Piers Gaveston returned to England following his third exile in early 1312 and was restored to his earldom of Cornwall, he and the king skulked in the north far away from their furious baronial opponents in the south. Edward II and Queen Isabella conceived their eldest child the future Edward III in about late February, shortly after the celebrations held in York to mark Joan Gaveston's birth and her mother Margaret's purification forty days after childbirth. On 5 April 1312, Edward and Gaveston left York for Newcastle, perhaps because it was much farther north and much farther from their baronial enemies, so they felt safer there. The pregnant Queen Isabella had joined them by 22 April, but soon moved on the 9 miles to Tynemouth Priory, because Gaveston was ill and might put her and her unborn child in danger. Edward's first cousin Thomas of Lancaster, one of Gaveston's most implacable enemies, had been moving slowly north, holding jousting tournaments along the way as a pretext to gather armed men. On 3 May, Edward and Gaveston learned of his imminent arrival at Newcastle, which took them completely by surprise. They fled to Tynemouth to join Isabella, escaping Lancaster by only a few hours and leaving most of Edward's household servants behind.

They left Tynemouth on 5 May, by sea, to the secure and fortified castle of Scarborough along the coast. As he and Gaveston would have to spend a few days in a small boat on the North Sea, a rough and bleak prospect, Edward II sent Queen Isabella by land instead, and they arranged to meet again at York a few days later. Isabella was in the first trimester of pregnancy, and she and the king decided that travelling by land would be a much safer option for her and her unborn child. A chronicler 270 miles away in St Albans, writing a few years later, wrote that Isabella begged Edward in tears not to leave her behind, but he callously abandoned her anyway, far more concerned with his beloved Piers Gaveston than with his wife and child. Although this story is often repeated as though it is true, the chronicler confused events of 1312 and 1322, and Isabella's household records reveal that she left Tynemouth at the same time as Edward and met up with him only a few days later in York. Her husband certainly did not abandon her sobbing and alone, though Isabella can hardly have been delighted that her lord and king skulked in the north and demonstrated time and again that Piers Gaveston was more important than almost anything and anyone else in his life.

The earl of Lancaster seized the baggage train of Edward II and Piers Gaveston which they had been forced to leave behind at Tynemouth, and which included a gold ring with an enormous ruby called 'the Cherry', and a gold cup studded with jewels bequeathed to the king by 'Queen Eleanor', either his mother Leonor of Castile, or his grandmother Eleanor of Provence, queen of Henry III. Also among the items the earl of Lancaster seized, which he returned to Edward a few months later – after the king had fumed that if anyone but a nobleman had taken his goods, that person 'could be found guilty of theft and rightly condemned by a verdict of robbery with violence' – were 'four silver forks for eating pears'. This is one of the earliest, if not the earliest, reference to forks in England, and it was centuries before they came into general use.

In October 1322, Isabella of France was once again at Tynemouth Priory; she stayed there while her husband unsuccessfully invaded

Scotland in August 1322, and for reasons which are inexplicable remained there even after Robert Bruce launched his counter-invasion of England some weeks later. The furious queen later accused Hugh Despenser the Younger of 'falsely and treacherously counselling the king to leave my lady the queen in peril of her person' at Tynemouth. Although Isabella seems genuinely to have believed this, and it was still clearly preying on her mind even four years later, Despenser did no such thing, and his own wife Eleanor, née de Clare, in fact was with the queen at Tynemouth, a fact which Isabella seems conveniently to have forgotten years later when she blamed Despenser for her predicament. Edward II, 90 miles away to the south, rushed off a number of letters to the constables of nearby castles ordering them to take his wife under their protection, and sent his household steward Sir Richard Damory and the earls of Richmond and Atholl with troops to her aid. No English chronicle so much as hints at the story, but a French chronicle claims that the men never reached her and that Isabella's household squires had to fortify Tynemouth Priory against Robert Bruce's men, and that the queen had to sail to safety down the coast. Supposedly two of her female attendants died during this journey.

It is difficult to take this tale particularly seriously – if the queen of England had truly been in danger from a Scottish army, some English chroniclers would certainly have realised and commented on it – but there is no doubt that Isabella of France did stay at Tynemouth Priory in the autumn of 1322. Her belief that she had been abandoned there at the say-so of Hugh Despenser the Younger, however inaccurate this belief was, was surely a major factor in a bad quarrel she and Edward had not long afterwards. Edward announced shortly before Christmas 1322 that his wife had gone on a pilgrimage to various sites around the country, which appears to be a politic excuse and a cover for her angry withdrawal from court.

To a point the royal couple reconciled, and were to spend time together and send each other gifts and letters while apart between 1323 and 1325. Their relationship – which had been mutually supportive and affectionate for almost fifteen years – had, however, been irrevocably damaged by what happened at Tynemouth Priory in October 1322, and by the king's relationship with Hugh Despenser the Younger. Isabella had always had considerable influence over her husband, gained a reputation as a mediator between the king and his barons, interceded with Edward on behalf of others, and was a powerful politician in her own right. That all ended abruptly in and after 1322, during the period when Hugh Despenser the Younger dominated Edward II and his government. Despenser seems to have gone out of his way to reduce Isabella's influence with her husband and even to remove her from the king's side, and Edward confiscated all of Isabella's lands in September 1324 when he went to war against her brother Charles IV of France, unkindly and unjustly treating his wife and the mother of his children as an enemy alien. Isabella loathed and feared Hugh Despenser to the extent that she claimed her life was in danger from him, and she resolved to destroy him. She achieved this in 1326; whether she had wished it or not, her destruction of Hugh Despenser the Younger brought her husband down as well. It is often wrongly assumed nowadays that Isabella of France hated and despised her husband and plotted for years to overthrow him and replace him with their son, but although she must have been furious about his confiscation of her lands, the notion that she hated Edward is based entirely on hindsight and assumption. Isabella's own letters reveal her great affection for her husband and her distress that Hugh Despenser the Younger had come between them and destroyed a marriage in which she had been happy. She called Edward her 'very sweet heart', and her 'very dear and very sweet lord and friend', and found her public opposition to him in late 1325 and 1326 painful and difficult. Had Edward sent Hugh Despenser the Younger away from him as Isabella demanded as her condition for her return to him from France in late 1325, English history would surely be very different; almost certainly Edward would have avoided his deposition of early 1327 and might then have reigned for many more years. The Hundred Years War between England and France began in the 1330s when Edward and Isabella's son, Edward III, claimed the French throne, and if Edward II had still been king then, this would not have happened, or at least would have played out very differently.

Although Edward II has a popular modern reputation as a gay king, and there is no doubt whatsoever that he loved men and almost certainly had sex with his male favourites, there is also no doubt that he was the father of all Isabella's children, and he fathered an illegitimate son as well, whom he named Adam. The identity of Adam's mother is not known, and it is not clear when he was born; probably sometime between 1305 and 1310 when Edward was 21 to 26 years old. Edward married Isabella of France on 25 January 1308, but as she was only 12 she could not become his wife in more than name for some years, and therefore

Edward's relationship that resulted in Adam took place either before his wedding or when Isabella was too young for him to consummate their marriage. Adam appears on record as 'Adam, bastard son of the lord king' during Edward's unsuccessful campaign to Scotland in August 1322, and appears to have been serving his father as a page or squire. He was accompanied by his tutor (magister) Hugh Chastillon. Dysentery swept through the royal army in August and September 1322, and perhaps Adam was a victim of it. His father buried his teenage son at Tynemouth Priory on 30 September 1322, paying for a silk cloth with gold thread to be laid over his body. Presumably his father would have arranged a marriage for him, and perhaps given him a manor or two, had he lived longer.

Tynemouth Priory and Castle are now owned and looked after by English Heritage, and stand on a headland next to the North Sea and the River Tyne, about nine miles from central Newcastle-upon-Tyne in the county of Tyne and Wear. The site can be reached by car, bus and the Newcastle Metro underground system. A thirteenth-century chapel that Edward II and Queen Isabella would have known still exists, as do the castle towers, gatehouse and keep.

Sheen (later Richmond Palace), London: One of Edward's Residences

In 1315 Edward II was given a manor in Surrey which was then called Shene, later spelt Sheen, and which at the end of the fifteenth century became known as Richmond Palace. In February 1313, an English nobleman called Edward Burnell granted the reversion of his manor of Sheen to his father-in-law Hugh Despenser the Elder, and Despenser must have given it to Edward II soon after it came into his hands on Burnell's death in August 1315; in December 1315, Edward called it 'the king's manor'. That month, he gave Sheen to twenty-four Carmelite friars, but in February 1318 moved them to a house just outside the north gate of Oxford instead, and retained Sheen for himself. Sheen stood on the River Thames west of London, and consisted of three islands and various dwellings.

From around 9 October 1325 until sometime in early 1326, Edward accommodated his niece Eleanor Despenser, née de Clare, at his manor of Sheen, and gave her a gift there of three swans and forty-seven caged goldfinches. She gave birth to a child, at least her tenth (this was probably her fifth daughter, Elizabeth Despenser, future Lady Berkeley), at Sheen in early December 1325, and Edward made an offering of thirty shillings to the Virgin Mary in gratitude that 'God granted [Eleanor] a prompt delivery of her child'. Edward went to visit Eleanor at Sheen and gave her a gift of 100 marks (£66) just after she gave birth – he rowed along the Thames from Westminster with eight attendants and returned the same day – and in early April 1325 had given her another gift of 100 marks at Beaulieu Abbey in Hampshire, apparently on hearing the news of her pregnancy. Eleanor Despenser was at Sheen again in early June 1326 and travelled from there to join the king at Kenilworth Castle in Warwickshire with her cousin John of Eltham, the king's younger son. Edward II often stayed at Sheen between 1324 and 1326. In the boiling hot, dry summer of 1326, the last of Edward's reign, he spent much time sailing along the River Thames west of London, and stayed at Sheen on several occasions. He and Eleanor Despenser, who spent all of that summer with him, gave alms to a group of fisherwomen whom they encountered one day near Sheen, and the king met a number of his subjects, talked to them and gave them gifts of money.

Somewhat peculiarly, a Flemish chronicler stated that Eleanor Despenser was involved in a sexual and incestuous affair with her uncle the king, and was imprisoned in the Tower of London after his downfall in late 1326 in case she was pregnant by him. This story cannot be confirmed and does not appear in any English chronicles, except one rather cryptic remark by a chronicler of Leicester that Eleanor Despenser behaved as though she were Edward's queen while Isabella of France was abroad in 1325/26. It is apparent from Edward's extant household accounts, however, that uncle and niece were extremely close indeed in the 1320s. Edward named one of his ships after his niece and frequently sent her letters, gifts and large sums of money; Eleanor reciprocated, and sent the king letters and gifts, including, on one occasion, a palfrey horse and on others, gifts of clothes. It cannot be proved that the two were lovers, but it is easy to understand why some contemporaries might have believed they were, just as there is evidence that Edward also had a physical relationship with her husband, Hugh Despenser the Younger. The Westminster chronicle *Flores Historiarum* commented in 1324 on Edward II's love of illicit and forbidden intimate relations.

Edward III had Sheen renovated and rebuilt, and died there in June 1377 at the age of 64; during the reign of his grandson Richard II, Sheen became a rather splendid royal palace. Richard's beloved queen, Anne of Bohemia, died there in June 1394, and ten months later a grieving Richard ordered the entire complex to be pulled down because he could no longer bear to spend time there without her. Henry V (r. 1413–22) rebuilt Sheen, often lived there and founded a priory nearby, and the first Tudor king, Henry VII (r. 1485–1509), rebuilt it again after a disastrous fire at the end of the 1400s and renamed it 'Richmond Palace', as he had been earl of Richmond (in Yorkshire) before he became king. Henry VIII's first child by Katherine of Aragon, Henry, duke of Cornwall, was born at Richmond Palace on 1 January 1511 and was baptised there, but died when he was only a few weeks old, and Henry's daughter, Queen Elizabeth I, died at Richmond in March 1603. The Stuart monarchs continued to use the palace, but much of it was demolished in the late seventeenth century, and three eighteenth-century buildings, now private residences, stand on the site.

Sheen, or Richmond Palace, stands on the south bank of the Thames, about 9 miles from the Palace of Westminster (now the Houses of Parliament; see below), in the London borough of Richmond. The gatehouse of the Tudor palace, the trumpeters' house and the wardrobe still exist, and there is a riverside walk along the Thames next to where Edward II's manor-house once stood. Nearby street names such as Old Palace Lane commemorate the vanished royal residence. Visitors can do what Edward II did on 2 December 1325 when he visited his niece Eleanor Despenser at Sheen by rowing himself along the Thames from Westminster; river boats can be hired, or for the less energetic, guided boat tours along the river are also available.

Westminster Abbey: The King Buys a Cottage

Around 1320, Edward II bought a cottage within the precincts of Westminster Abbey and called it Borgoyne or 'Burgundy'. According to the disgruntled monk of Westminster who wrote the chronicle *Flores Historiarum* ('Flowers of History') and who loathed Edward and frequently ranted about him and his 'insane stupidity', the king's possession of the cottage was 'not without sacrilege'. Edward II, who for all faults never lacked a sense of humour, supposedly referred to himself jocularly as 'the king of Burgundy'. He spent much of February and

March 1325 at his cottage, and two squires of his household – Giles of Spain and Burgeys de Tilh from Gascony in south-west France – performed some kind of act in the hall of the cottage for his entertainment, involving fire. Unfortunately, the trick went wrong, and the two men burned themselves quite badly; Edward gave them the equivalent of a year's wages each in compensation. During the hot summer of 1326, Edward hired a group of twenty-seven workmen to dig ditches around his cottage of Burgundy, bought them drinks, and watched them work (and might have picked up a spade and joined in, as he did at Clarendon Palace soon afterwards).

The exact location of Edward II's cottage at Westminster is unfortunately not known, but it stood somewhere next to Westminster Abbey, and the abbey was also a significant place in Edward's life. His grandfather Henry III and parents Edward I and Leonor of Castile were buried in the chapel of St Edward the Confessor inside the abbey, and Edward himself was crowned king of England there, with his young bride Isabella of France at his side, on 25 February 1308. Edward held parliaments yearly or thereabouts, and when he was not in York or Lincoln the parliaments took place at Westminster or London. The king often stayed at his palace of Westminster, at the Tower of London a couple of miles away, and at his manor-house of Sheen. He spent the night at his cottage of 'Burgundy' quite often in 1325/26, with only a few attendants; perhaps he enjoyed the privacy.

Westminster in Edward II's time, and long before and afterwards, stood outside the city of London, and was reached by the road called the Strand, where rich nobles owned large and expensive riverside properties. Nowadays, Westminster stands in the middle of a mega-city, and is so clogged with traffic and people that it is more or less impossible to imagine what it might have looked like in the fourteenth century. Where the Houses of Parliament now stand was once a great palace, the Palace of Westminster; indeed, the official name of the Houses of Parliament is still the 'Palace of Westminster'. The great medieval palace burned down in 1834, and must once have been a splendid sight. There are mentions in Edward II's accounts of the Painted Chamber within the palace which had been built by his grandfather Henry III, and Edward himself contributed to its rich and vividly decorated walls by having scenes from the life of his father painted on them in the 1320s. Edward's eldest niece Eleanor de Clare married Hugh Despenser the Younger in the Palace of Westminster on 26 May 1306 in the presence of her grandfather Edward I and her uncle the future Edward II; the wedding is likely to have taken place in the chapel of St Stephen, which stood next to the Painted Chamber.

Days before this wedding, on 22 May 1306, the future King Edward II – then Prince of Wales, duke of Aquitaine, count of Ponthieu and earl of Chester, and 22 years old – was knighted in a private ceremony in Westminster Palace by his father. Later that day, he personally knighted 266 other young men inside Westminster Abbey, including his beloved Piers Gaveston; his future beloved Hugh Despenser the Younger, who became his nephew-in-law four days later; Roger Mortimer of Wigmore, who would bring him down in 1326/27; and John Maltravers of Dorset, who would be one of his custodians at Berkeley Castle in 1327 after his deposition. Edward of Caernarfon appears on the list of new knights as *Dominus Edwardus Princeps Walliae*, 'Lord Edward, Prince of Wales'. After the ceremony, the 267 young knights made their way from the abbey into Westminster Hall, where a great banquet called the 'Feast of the Swan' took place. (Two minstrels bore in a plate bearing two large swans, though whether they were real animals or recreated ones is not clear.) Edward I spared no expense on the minstrels who entertained his son and his fellow new knights. They included the famous acrobat Matilda Makejoy, Pearl in the Eye (who had cataracts), Edward of Caernarfon's trumpeters Januche and Gillot, his harper Amekyn, Reginald 'the Liar' (i.e. a storyteller of fantastic tales), and one called simply 'the minstrel with the bells'.

Westminster Abbey dates back more than 1,000 years. The present church was founded by Edward the Confessor (d. 1066), king of England and later a saint, in the 1040s when he had a royal palace built on Thorney Island near London and converted a nearby Benedictine monastery into the 'west minster'. The name distinguished it from the 'east minster', i.e. St Paul's Cathedral. Edward the Confessor's church was consecrated on 28 December 1065, just days before he died, and almost exactly a year later on Christmas Day 1066, William the Conqueror became the first king of England to be crowned at Westminster. All the kings and queens of England since, with the exceptions of the uncrowned Edward V in 1483, Jane Grey in 1553, and Edward VIII who abdicated before his coronation in 1936, have followed. The present building was considerably renovated and rebuilt in the thirteenth century by Edward II's grandfather Henry III. Henry, his sons Edward I and Edmund of Lancaster, and his daughter-in-law Leonor of Castile were all buried in Westminster Abbey, and their tombs can still be seen. Edward II himself – deposed and disgraced – was buried in distant Gloucester and not at Westminster, but his son Edward III and daughter-in-law Philippa of Hainault, and great-grandson Richard II and Richard's queen, Anne of Bohemia, lie there. The tomb and gorgeous alabaster effigy of Edward II's second son John of Eltham, earl of Cornwall, can also still be seen in the abbey. John died unmarried and childless in Perth, Scotland, in September 1336 at the age of 20; his mother Isabella of France outlived him by more than twenty years. Small statues, some of them wearing crowns, were carved around the base of the tomb as 'weepers', and represent members of John's family, including his parents.

Westminster Abbey is open to visitors every week from Monday to Saturday; Sundays and holy days are reserved for worship. Tickets can be purchased at the door or in advance online. Westminster Hall, which dates to 1097 and has a magnificent and rightly famous hammer-beam roof built by Richard II in the 1390s, can be seen as part of a tour of the Houses of Parliament, on Saturdays and on weekdays during parliamentary recesses. Tickets can also be purchased online.

The Tower of London: Birthplace of Edward's Second Daughter

Unlike many other medieval English kings, most notably his father, Edward II did not spend much money renovating, rebuilding and improving the Tower of London, though he did spend quite a lot of time here, especially between 1324 and 1326. His and Isabella of France's youngest child, Joan of the Tower, queen of Robert Bruce's son and successor, David II of Scotland, was born here on 5 July 1321. Edward was elsewhere in London on the day his daughter was born, and gave the man who brought him the news a gift of £80. He subsequently stayed at the Tower with his wife Isabella and their baby daughter for a few days. A few weeks after little Joan's birth, Edward and Hugh Despenser the Younger's baronial enemies the Contrariants arrived for parliament, placed their armies around the walls of London to prevent the king and Despenser leaving, and demanded the perpetual exile of Despenser and his father.

After Edward's successful campaign against the Contrariants, his enemies Roger Mortimer of Wigmore (b. 1286/7) and Mortimer's namesake uncle Roger Mortimer of Chirk (b. c. 1256) submitted to him at Shrewsbury, and in February 1322 the two men were sent to the Tower of London to be imprisoned. Mortimer of Wigmore escaped from the Tower on 1 August 1323, one of the few men in history to do so, and fled to the Continent; his uncle Mortimer of Chirk died still imprisoned in the Tower in August 1326, at the age of about 70. Mortimer of Wigmore joined other exiled Contrariants on the Continent, and in early 1326 they visited the French court and allied with Edward II's queen Isabella of France, who had openly declared her fear and loathing of Hugh Despenser the Younger and her intention to destroy him. Edward II was staying at the Tower of London on 27 September 1326 when he heard that Isabella and her invasion force, including Roger Mortimer of Wigmore and other survivors of the Contrariant faction of 1321/22, had arrived at the River Orwell in Suffolk three days earlier. On the day of the invasion force's arrival, the oblivious king had himself gone out to the postern gate of the Tower and paid a passing fisherman called Richard Marbon three shillings for two salmon.

Nowadays, the famous building The Shard thrusts its way up into the sky opposite the River Thames, and HMS *Belfast* is permanently moored in the river near the Tower. In Edward II's time, the cityscape of course looked rather different. Tower Bridge did not exist in the fourteenth century or for hundreds of years afterwards, and the only bridge across the Thames in London that Edward would have known was London Bridge. His capital had perhaps 50,000 inhabitants; 700 years later it has close to 9 million. If Edward could travel through time to the twenty-first century, he would certainly recognise some of the Tower as it exists today, but virtually nothing else.

In late 1324 and early 1325, Edward II bought three houses opposite the Tower in Southwark, not far from where The Shard now stands and very close to the site now occupied by City Hall; two of the houses were called La Rosere and La Cage, and the name of the third was not recorded. The king had them renovated, rebuilt and plastered, and he connected La Rosere and La Cage with a covered walkway, had flowers and shrubs planted in the gardens, and had the kitchen of La Rosere plastered and tiled. There is some evidence from Edward's household accounts that he intended his London houses to be something of a private refuge and a getaway from his enormous household – at least 500 people – and from all the earls, barons, knights and bishops who permanently attended him. His cottage of Burgundy at Westminster was probably used in the same way. Edward had his own chamber on an upper floor of La Rosere, and used the house as the venue for a discreet assignation with an unnamed lover during the parliament held in London and Westminster in October 1324; a fisherman of London was paid two shillings to carry Edward across the Thames from the Tower to La Rosere, and two of Edward's chamber clerks bought a quantity of fish, seafood, butter and onions for the king and his lover after he 'secretly took his pleasure' there.

Edward II's houses of La Rosere and La Cage have long since disappeared, but the Tower still stands in central London, and is open to the public every day except 24–26 December and 1 January. In the fourteenth century it had not yet acquired the sinister reputation it enjoyed in Tudor times, when several prominent prisoners such as Anne Boleyn and Katherine Howard were beheaded within its walls. In Edward II's time it was already often used as a prison, but was also a royal residence and, curiously, a menagerie founded by Edward II's grandfather Henry III, after his brother-in-law Louis IX of France gave him an elephant in 1254. Edward himself kept lions and leopards here. The name 'the Tower of London' is something of a misnomer, as it contains over twenty towers and is an enormous sprawling fortification covering 12 acres. Three towers – Lanthorn, St Thomas's and Wakefield – are collectively known nowadays as the Medieval Palace, and in St Thomas's Tower there is a reconstruction of Edward I's bedchamber, as he and his son Edward II would have known it.

Oriel College, Oxford: Edward's Foundation

Despite the huge stress he was under in early 1326 after learning that his own queen was allying with his baronial enemies, Roger Mortimer of Wigmore and the other Contrariants in exile on the Continent, Edward II found time to establish a college at the University of Oxford. His almoner, Adam Brome, officially founded the college in the king's name on 21 January 1326, and the foundation charter says that love of the Blessed Virgin Mary and a desire to increase her 'divine cult' motivated Edward to establish the college. The king also declared his zeal for sound learning and religious knowledge. The foundation was originally named the 'Hall of the Blessed Mary'; the name 'Oriel' comes from a house called La Oriole granted to the college by Edward III some years later, after Edward II's deposition. La Oriole had a projecting upper window, an oriel window, hence the name.

Even today, Oriel's startlingly long official full name is 'The Provost and Scholars of the House of the Blessed Mary the Virgin in Oxford, commonly called Oriel College, of the foundation of Edward the Second of famous memory, sometime king of England'. It is one of the thirty-eight constituent colleges of the university, and the fifth oldest surviving college at Oxford after University, Balliol, Merton and Exeter. Famous Oriel alumni include Sir Walter Raleigh, the Regency dandy Beau Brummell, the poet Matthew Arnold (elected a Fellow in 1845), Cecil Rhodes, and Winston Churchill's grandfather, John Spencer-Churchill, duke of Marlborough. The college is generally open to tourists in the afternoons at a small charge, except during the Trinity or summer term. A virtual tour is available on the college website.

Edward II's close ally Walter Stapeldon, elected Bishop of Exeter in 1307 and twice appointed Treasurer of England by the king in the 1320s, founded Exeter College at Oxford in 1314, the fourth oldest college of the university. It was originally known as Stapeldon Hall, and its famous alumni include J.R.R. Tolkien, actor Richard Burton and athlete Roger Bannister. The unfortunate Walter Stapeldon was murdered in London on 15 October 1326 after Queen Isabella's invasion force arrived in Suffolk and the capital exploded into chaos. Stapeldon, seen as an ally of the hated Hugh Despenser the Younger and his father, was a prime target, and was caught by a mob while trying to flee inside St Paul's Cathedral to seek sanctuary. He was beheaded with a bread knife, and his head sent to the queen. His tomb can still be seen in Exeter Cathedral.

A royal palace stood in the city of Oxford in the Middle Ages which Edward II gave to the order of Carmelite friars (the 'White Friars') in 1318. This was in fulfilment of a vow he had made just after the battle of Bannockburn. Either as a plea to God to save him from capture by the Scots, or in gratitude that he had evaded capture, Edward swore to found a Carmelite friary. In February 1318, he granted the Carmelites his Beaumont Palace in Oxford, and by 1324 had also granted them plots of land covering 7½ acres and permission to construct a 'subterraneous way' under the king's highway, 50ft long and 10ft wide, to connect their buildings. The Carmelites promised in return to celebrate divine service daily for Edward, Queen Isabella and their children for their whole lives and after death, and for the souls of Edward's ancestors.

Soon after this grant, a man called John of Powderham or John Deydras ordered the Carmelites to 'leave his house'. He was a royal impostor who claimed to be the rightful son of Edward I, and had, unbeknownst to the king, taken up residence at Beaumont Palace. News of this claim came to Edward II's ears, and Powderham was arrested and brought before him. Edward, who never lacked a sense of humour, greeted him with the ironic words 'Welcome, my brother'. Powderham exclaimed that 'my lord Edward … was not of the blood royal, nor had any right to the realm', because he himself was Edward I's true son. He had been attacked, he claimed, by a wild pig while lying in his cradle as a baby, and his nurse, too afraid to tell the king that his son had been maimed and his ear torn off, substituted him with a peasant baby. There was no truth at all to Powderham's claim to be royal, but his story was given widespread credence; most people found it hard to accept that their king preferred hedging, ditching, fishing and swimming to governing, fighting and jousting, and believed Powderham, 'all the more readily because the said lord Edward resembled the elder lord Edward [I] in none of his virtues.' One chronicle says that Edward II wished to make John of Powderham his court jester, but that the great magnates insisted on his execution.

Edward's great-great-great-great-grandfather, Henry I, had Beaumont Palace built in the early 1130s, three years after he had Woodstock built a few miles away. Henry stayed there at Easter 1132, and the following year held great celebrations at Beaumont to mark the birth of his grandson, the future Henry II. Henry I's great-grandsons King Richard Lionheart and King John, sons of Henry II and Eleanor of Aquitaine, were born there in 1157 and 1166 respectively. By 1308, the palace was apparently in a somewhat ruinous state, as on 22 April that year Edward II ordered the sheriff of Oxfordshire to repair the towers, walls and houses of Oxford Castle by using stone and timber from his palace in Oxford, i.e. Beaumont. The Carmelite friary of Oxford was closed down during the Dissolution, and although some ruins remained in 1785, when an engraving of the former palace was made, Beaumont Street was laid out on the site in 1828 and now nothing of it remains. An inscription on a pillar on the street recalls the palace: 'Near to this site stood the king's houses later known as Beaumont Palace.' The famous Ashmolean Museum, the world's oldest university museum which was founded in 1683, stands on Beaumont Street, opposite the site where a royal palace once stood.

Chapter Four

Deposition and Aftermath, 1326–1330

Tintern Abbey, Monmouthshire, Wales:
Visited by the King in Flight

Standing on the border of Monmouthshire in Wales and Gloucestershire in England, Tintern Abbey is the second-oldest Cistercian foundation in the country, and Edward II and Hugh Despenser the Younger stayed here on 14 and 15 October 1326 during their flight towards Wales from Edward's wife Isabella's invasion force. Despenser and Edward left London at the beginning of October 1326, realising that they could not possibly hold Edward's hostile capital and might easily be trapped there by the invasion force (as they had been by the Contrariants' armies in August 1321). They made for South Wales, which was almost entirely owned and controlled by Despenser, looking for aid and support. Little came; Despenser's tyranny and the king's support of it ensured that men either stayed away, or joined Isabella. Despenser's father, Hugh Despenser the Elder, earl of Winchester, was captured in Bristol on 27 October and hanged in his armour, and the Despensers' close ally Edmund Fitzalan, earl of Arundel, whose son and heir Richard was married to Despenser the Younger's eldest daughter Isabella, was beheaded without a trial in Hereford on 17 November 1326, the day after the king and Despenser were captured near Llantrisant. The earl of Arundel's cousin, Roger Mortimer, oversaw his execution, and seems to have deliberately ordered it to be done with a blunt axe: the executioner needed somewhere between seventeen and twenty-two strokes to sever the unfortunate earl of Arundel's head.

Tintern was founded in 1131 by Walter de Clare, lord of Chepstow, a member of the same powerful aristocratic family as Edward II's nieces Eleanor, Margaret and Elizabeth de Clare (though he was not their direct ancestor). Only Waverley Abbey in Surrey, founded in 1128, is an older Cistercian foundation in Britain. The Cistercians or 'White Monks' were a strict and austere order who built their abbeys in remote valleys, and the order became hugely popular across England and Wales in the twelfth and thirteenth centuries. One of Tintern Abbey's most generous benefactors was Roger Bigod, earl of Norfolk and lord of Chepstow (c. 1245-1306), who was the step-grandfather of Hugh Despenser the Younger; Bigod's first wife Aline Despenser, née Basset, who died in 1281, was the mother of Hugh Despenser the Elder from her first marriage. Bigod paid for the abbey church to be rebuilt at the end of the thirteenth century, a major undertaking. Much of it still remains.

In 1317, Edward II arranged the marriage of his twice-widowed niece Elizabeth de Burgh, née de Clare, to his current court favourite Sir Roger Damory, a knight of Oxfordshire who had served in the retinue of Elizabeth's brother Gilbert de Clare, earl of Gloucester. Damory fought at Bannockburn, and although his lord the earl of Gloucester was killed there, Damory himself was later rewarded by Edward II for his valour on the battlefield. From 1315 until early 1319 Damory was extremely influential at Edward's court, and became wealthy and influential as a result of the king's infatuation with him, but was ousted from the king's side by his brother-in-law and great rival Hugh Despenser the Younger. Damory joined the Contrariant rebellion against Edward and Despenser in 1321/22, and died of wounds sustained while fighting against the royal army on 12 or 13 March 1322. By right of his wife Elizabeth, Roger Damory controlled the lordships of Usk and Caerleon near Tintern Abbey, and became its patron.

Tintern Abbey was dissolved in 1536, but almost 500 years later, extensive and beautiful ruins survive. In 1798, the famous Romantic poet William Wordsworth visited the area, and was inspired to write a short poem titled 'Lines written a few miles above Tintern Abbey'. It is now looked after by Cadw, the historic environment service of the Welsh government, and is open most days of the year.

Caerphilly Castle, Caerphilly County Borough, South Wales: Edward's Refuge

Caerphilly Castle, 8 miles from Wales's largest city and capital, Cardiff, is one of the biggest castles in Britain and one of the great medieval castles of Europe. Edward II sought refuge here for a few days shortly before his capture on 16 November 1326. Now located in the centre of the town of Caerphilly, it was built in the early 1270s by the hugely wealthy and influential English nobleman Gilbert 'the Red' de Clare (1243–95), earl of Gloucester and Hertford, who became Edward of Caernarfon's brother-in-law in April 1290 when he married Edward's much older sister Joan of Acre. Gilbert designed and built his castle in the interests of conquering Glamorgan and making himself its lord, and to counter the power of Llywelyn ap Gruffudd (c. 1223–82), Prince of Wales. He introduced concentric castle design to Britain in his construction of Caerphilly, and in its heyday it was surrounded by extensive artificial lakes and was virtually impregnable. It was, and remains, a masterpiece of castle design, and remarkably, with the exception of some later improvements and additions, was built in under three years; even an attack on the site by Llywelyn ap Gruffudd in 1270 did not cause much disruption or delay. As well as being an ingeniously designed stronghold, however, it was also built to provide a comfortable home for Gilbert and his family, and his daughter Eleanor Despenser, née de Clare, was born there in October 1292. Most of what can be seen today was built by Gilbert; his son-in-law Hugh Despenser the Younger, lord of Glamorgan, remodelled the great hall and other domestic buildings. Despenser and Edward II spent a few days at Caerphilly from 27 October until 2 November 1326, shortly before their capture and Despenser's execution; Despenser's eldest son and heir Hugh, Edward II's great-nephew and Gilbert the Red's grandson, was besieged here from November 1326 to March 1327 on the orders of Edward's queen Isabella.

During a rebellion against English rule in 1294, the Welshman Morgan ap Maredudd attacked Caerphilly but was unable to take it, though he did burn the small town which had grown up outside the castle. Caerphilly was attacked again twenty-two years later by the Welsh lord Llywelyn Bren. Llywelyn and his people were furious at the high-handed behaviour of Sir Payn Turberville, the royal official ruling Glamorgan after the young earl of Gloucester's death at the battle of Bannockburn, and he launched an attack on Caerphilly on 26 January 1316. Although Bren could not penetrate the inner ward of the impregnable castle, he burned the outer ward, took the custodian captive, killed some servants and wounded others. As in 1294, the small town outside the castle walls was burned. Bren and his many supporters – said to number 10,000 – carried off Payn Turberville's goods into the mountains where they were hiding, and Bren threatened to kill the hated official. The news took a few days to travel the more than 200 miles from Caerphilly to Lincoln where Edward II was holding parliament, and when the king finally heard on 7 February 1316, he immediately sent men to capture Bren and nip his rebellion in the bud, exclaiming: 'Go quickly, and pursue this traitor, lest from delay worse befall us and all Wales rise against us.' Sir William Montacute, Sir Hugh Audley, Sir Roger Damory, the king's cousin Henry of Lancaster and his brother-in-law the earl of Hereford, Roger Mortimer of Wigmore and the others soon succeeded, and Bren, his wife Lleucu and his six sons were imprisoned in the Tower of London. Llywelyn Bren was executed, probably by hanging, drawing and quartering, at Cardiff in or soon after 1318.

In April 1317 almost three years after his nephew the earl of Gloucester, Gilbert the Red's son and heir, fell at Bannockburn, Edward II ordered the earl's vast estate to be partitioned among his heirs. In the division of the Clare inheritance in November 1317, the lordship of Glamorgan, including Caerphilly Castle, passed to the late Earl Gilbert's sister Eleanor and her husband Hugh Despenser the Younger. Eleanor was Edward's eldest and favourite niece, and high in his favour throughout his reign, unlike her younger sisters Margaret and Elizabeth, who both suffered imprisonment after their husbands, Hugh Audley and Roger Damory, joined the Contrariant rebellion against the king and Despenser in 1321/22.

Whatever may have been going on between Edward II and Eleanor and Hugh Despenser came to an end in early October 1326, shortly after Edward's queen Isabella invaded his kingdom and landed at the River Orwell in Suffolk. Edward left the Tower of London in Eleanor's control, and headed towards Glamorgan with Hugh Despenser, Despenser's father the earl of Winchester, and their ally Edmund Fitzalan, earl of Arundel. Hugh the Younger owned Glamorgan, and Edward had always been more popular in Wales, his birthplace, than in England, and they therefore hoped to raise troops and repel the invasion. It was not to be. They left Despenser's father in Bristol, where he was captured and executed on 27 October 1326, and the earl of Arundel was executed in Hereford on 17 November. Edward and Despenser arrived at Caerphilly Castle on 27 October, the day of the earl of Winchester's execution, and left again on 2 November for reasons which remain mysterious. The castle was well provisioned for a siege, and they had a huge amount of money with them: £1,000 of Despenser's in one barrel, and £13,000 of the king's in twenty-six barrels.

When the king and Despenser, inexplicably, left the safety of Caerphilly on 2 November 1326, many of the king's chamber staff remained within, while Edward and Despenser set off for Neath Abbey. They were captured probably near Llantrisant on Sunday, 16 November 1326, apparently on their way back to Caerphilly. Had they been able to reach the safety of the massive fortification, perhaps they would have been able to negotiate a different outcome with Queen Isabella and her many allies, but as it was, Despenser was taken to Hereford to be executed on 24 November, and Edward himself was sent to his cousin Henry of Lancaster's castle of Kenilworth in Warwickshire. Unlike Despenser, the king was treated with respect and honour, though his reign came to an end in all but name on the day of his capture.

Despenser's eldest son and heir, yet another Hugh Despenser (known to his family by the nickname 'Huchon'), was born in 1308 or the first half of 1309; he was the eldest great-grandchild of Edward I, and spent much of the last years of his great-uncle Edward II's reign at court. He was left behind in the castle built by his grandfather Gilbert 'the Red' when his father and Edward II departed. Sometime in November 1326, Queen Isabella and her allies sent a large force of men to besiege the castle, consisting of twenty-five knights, twenty-one squires, 400 footmen, and others. Inside Caerphilly were approximately 135 men, though only two of them were knights and there was a mere handful of other fighting men, most were carpenters, blacksmiths, fishermen, household staff, and so on. As well as many former members of Edward II's household, the Caerphilly garrison of 1326/27 included the master carpenter William Hurley, who worked on Ely Cathedral, Windsor Castle, and the palace of Westminster as well as on the great hall of Caerphilly Castle. Despenser and Edward had left Caerphilly under the command of Sir John Felton, who was not its official constable but was one of Despenser's retainers, and he swore an oath to them on the Gospels not to give the castle up to the queen or her eldest son. This was the 14-year-old Edward of Windsor, who succeeded his deposed father as King Edward III in January 1327. In November 1326, Hugh 'Huchon' Despenser was only 17 or 18 and had committed no crime, but he was the hated Hugh Despenser the Younger's eldest son and heir, and Queen Isabella wished to execute him as she had his father and grandfather. To lead the siege of Caerphilly, Queen Isabella appointed the baron William de la Zouche, lord of Ashby in Leicestershire, and one of the men who had captured Hugh Despenser the Younger and Edward II near Llantrisant. Over the next few months, she frequently offered the entire garrison free pardons if they surrendered the young Despenser inside for execution. Bravely, the garrison refused to give the young man up.

On 20 March 1327, the queen finally gave in, and agreed to spare the young Despenser's life. The garrison duly surrendered and were all pardoned, while Huchon Despenser was imprisoned until July 1331 and finally released after his cousin Edward III had overthrown his mother Isabella and her ally Roger Mortimer in October 1330 and begun ruling his kingdom himself. Huchon Despenser spent the next few years doing his utmost to restore the Despenser family's good name, made an excellent marriage to the earl of Salisbury's daughter Elizabeth, fought bravely in the early years of the Hundred Years War, and died in February 1349, possibly of the Black Death. He was buried in Tewkesbury Abbey, Gloucestershire, with his parents; see elsewhere in this volume for more details.

A careful and exceedingly long inventory was taken of all the goods left inside Caerphilly Castle after it finally surrendered on 20 March 1327. The list of items runs to a few pages, and included Edward II's luxurious bed with a counterpane of red silk lined with green silk and a warm coverlet lined with miniver fur, four purple and four red velvet cushions, two urinals in a chest also for the king's use, a black cap lined with red velvet and embroidered with pearls in the shape of butterflies and 'diverse beasts', 1,130 crossbow bolts, and a red and saffron striped robe embroidered with bears, 'for the king's retiring'. The stores of food included one tun of oatmeal, almost 300 carcasses of mutton and seventy-eight of oxen, seventy-two hams, three tuns each of vinegar and honey, six tuns of red wine and one of white 'whereof 10 inches are lacking', and 1,856 stockfish. (One pities the poor soul given the thankless task of counting the stockfish and the crossbow bolts.) This was after a siege of at least four months, so Despenser the Younger had left his castle well provisioned indeed.

At the command of Hugh Despenser the Younger, the carpenter William Hurley and his team remodelled the great hall of Caerphilly between about 1322 and 1326. What can be seen there today dates from Despenser's time, except the roof which was rebuilt in the nineteenth century. The hall is an impressive 20 metres long and over 10 metres wide, and is entered nowadays via the inner ward. One very interesting feature of the great hall is the number of stone corbels, which were carved into faces (corbels are projections jutting out from a wall, supporting a heavy structure above). One depicts a bearded man wearing a crown, almost certainly intended to be Edward II. The stone face next to his seems extremely likely, therefore, to be a depiction of Hugh Despenser the Younger, and although the features have worn away over the centuries, it seems to show him with long hair, a goatee-style beard and an oval, perhaps rather plump, face. Other corbels surely represent Despenser's wife Eleanor de Clare and other members of their family, and one is probably Edward II's Queen Isabella, who had Despenser and his father executed and his widow imprisoned in the Tower of London for fifteen months. After spending a great deal of money improving the private accommodation at Caerphilly, and personalising it, Despenser himself had no time or opportunity to enjoy it.

Hugh 'Huchon' Despenser succeeded as lord of Glamorgan and owner of Caerphilly Castle on the death of his mother Eleanor, née de Clare, in 1337, and when he died childless in 1349, the castle passed to his nephew Edward Despenser (1336–75). It remained in the Despenser family until the 1420s, when Hugh the Younger and Eleanor de Clare's great-great-granddaughter and heir Isabelle Despenser married Richard Beauchamp, earl of Warwick, and in 1486 Henry VII granted it to his uncle Jasper Tudor. The siege of Huchon Despenser in 1326/27 was, however, the last excitement Caerphilly Castle saw, and it fell into a long decline and was already ruinous in the late 1530s when the antiquarian John Leland visited it. By the time of the Civil War in the 1640s, Caerphilly was far too dilapidated to be able to serve any purpose as a fortification, though it was sympathetically restored for posterity by the Marquis of Bute in the nineteenth century, and today presents a spectacular and dramatic sight for visitors. Caerphilly Castle is now looked after by Cadw, and is open to the public daily except for 24, 25 and 26 December and 1 January, at a cost of a few pounds. Hugh Despenser the Younger's great hall can be booked for weddings and other events; details and prices can be found on the Cadw website.

Llantrisant Castle, Rhondda Cynon Taf, South Wales: Edward's Temporary Prison

After Edward II left Caerphilly Castle on 2 November 1326 with most of the household staff who had not yet abandoned him inside, his movements become much more difficult to ascertain, but he and Hugh Despenser the Younger certainly went to Neath Abbey for some days, and were captured somewhere near Llantrisant on Sunday, 16 November. Chroniclers narrate that the king and his chamberlain were captured during a violent thunderstorm which lasted most of the day, a story which would sound like dramatic licence were it not that two of them, who could not have been influenced by each other, give the same tale. (Another English chronicler, ignorant of Welsh geography, states that the king was captured 'near Snowdon' in North Wales.) Edward and Despenser were under 10 miles from Caerphilly Castle and presumably were on their way back there after wandering to Neath. Only a handful of men remained with them; the king of England had been abandoned by almost everyone, and it must have been painfully, humiliatingly apparent to him that his support had entirely collapsed.

Edward and Despenser either tried to seek refuge in Llantrisant Castle – which, like most of the rest of South Wales, belonged to Despenser himself – or, more probably, were taken there briefly after their capture. A place still known locally as Pant-y-Brad, the 'Vale of Treachery' or 'Hollow of Treason', has traditionally been assumed to be the location where Edward and Despenser were taken by a search party. This party included two of the sons of the Welsh rebel Llywelyn Bren who had been executed in Cardiff in 1318, Henry of Lancaster, who was both Edward's cousin and Despenser's brother-in-law, and William de la Zouche, who would besiege Despenser's son inside Caerphilly Castle, and abduct and marry Despenser's widow Eleanor in early 1329.

All that remains now of Llantrisant, the temporary prison of the disgraced Edward II in November 1326, is a ruinous tower covered with ivy. The castle was built in the middle of the thirteenth century by Richard de Clare, earl of Gloucester and lord of Glamorgan, father of Gilbert 'the Red', and grandfather of Hugh Despenser the Younger's wife Eleanor. Richard's daughter Margaret (c. 1249–1312), who married Edmund, earl of Cornwall, was born in the castle, and with the rest of the lordship of Glamorgan, it passed to Hugh and Eleanor in 1317. Llantrisant was one of the many castles and manors which the Marcher lords, or Contrariants, attacked during the Despenser War of May 1321, and after Edward and Despenser emerged victorious over the Contrariants in March 1322, they had one Sir William Fleming hanged. Fleming had been keeper of Llantrisant Castle before Despenser inherited it, and was also keeper of the land of Glamorgan in 1317 and of the Gower peninsula (which Edward gave to Despenser in 1322) in 1320. Presumably, Fleming angered Despenser in some way.

Although not much of the once mighty castle still exists, the tower gives an impression of menacing power, and the site commands stunning views over the Vale of Glamorgan and the coastline of northern Devon in the distance. Cadw now looks after the site, and it can easily be visited in combination with some of Hugh Despenser's other magnificent South Wales castles such as Caerphilly, Cardiff, Newport and Neath.

Hereford, Herefordshire: Edward's Beloved Despenser is Executed

Hugh Despenser the Younger was grotesquely executed in the city of Hereford on 24 November 1326, in the presence of the woman who loathed him and had sworn to destroy him: Queen Isabella. Edward II's wife had made a speech to the French court in late October 1325 describing Despenser as a 'Pharisee' and an 'intruder' who had come between herself and her husband and destroyed their marriage. She gave Edward an ultimatum; send Despenser away so that she could return to him and resume their marriage, or she would remain in France and not permit their son Edward of Windsor to return to his father either. Edward simply refused to send Despenser away from him, which left Isabella no choice but to remain in France and ally with Despenser's enemies on the Continent, the remnant of the Contrariant faction of 1321/22. It took her only a year to achieve her vow to destroy Hugh Despenser the Younger.

After the capture of the king and Despenser on 16 November 1326, Despenser refused all food and drink, presumably trying to kill himself in the only way he could before he was subjected to the most savage execution possible. A crown of nettles was placed on his head, he was tied to a mean horse, with his ally Simon of Reading forced to go before him with his coat of arms reversed, and led slowly to Hereford. The 60-mile journey took over a week. All the way, squires blew bugle horns constantly in Despenser's ears, and the populace pelted him with filth, rubbish, and verbal abuse. On arrival in Hereford, Biblical verses including 'Why do you glory in wrong-doing?' were scrawled over his skin. In front of Hereford Castle – which belonged to Despenser personally – a show trial took place which consisted of a list of charges being read out by a lawyer called Sir William Trussell. Besides Queen Isabella, also present in Hereford on 24 November 1326 were the queen's uncle and the king's first cousin Henry of Lancaster (who was Despenser's brother-in-law, the widower of his half-sister Maud), Edward II's half-brothers the earls of Norfolk and Kent, Isabella's ally Roger Mortimer of Wigmore, the other Contrariants who had taken part in the invasion, Hugh Audley, another of Despenser's brothers-in-law and imprisoned as a Contrariant in 1322, and many others.

The charges against Despenser were numerous; some were more or less accurate, others contained enough of a kernel of truth to seem vaguely plausible, and others were absolutely absurd, simply propaganda which heaped all of Edward II's errors and failures on Despenser's head. He was condemned to death by hanging, drawing and quartering and dragged by four horses through the streets of Hereford to the market-place, where he was hanged on a pre-built gallows 50ft high, before being cut down, disembowelled and castrated. Finally, his head was cut off. It is not impossible that Edward II was in Hereford during Despenser's trial and execution, as his custodian and cousin Henry of Lancaster was certainly there, though presumably he was not made to witness the execution as no chronicler mentions the king's presence. Despenser's head was carried down Cheapside in London on 4 or 6 December 1326 and placed on a spike on London Bridge, and his body was hacked into four quarters and publicly displayed in York, Carlisle, Bristol and Dover for four years.

Sadly nothing at all remains of Hereford Castle where a royal favourite's show trial took place on 24 November 1326; the ruins were knocked down in the mid-eighteenth century, and now a recreation area called Castle Green stands on the site. Hereford was one of the very few English castles which pre-dated the Norman Conquest, and dated back to the early 1050s. The area where Despenser was executed is now a pedestrianised square and shopping area in the centre of the city; a building nearby called the Black and White House dates back to 1621 and is now a museum. The city of Hereford stands on the River Wye, 23 miles from Gloucester where

Edward II is buried, and its name probably derives from the Old English word for 'army' coupled with 'ford', i.e. a river crossing. It lies close to the Welsh border, and the Battle of Hereford took place there in 760 between armies of the Anglo–Saxon kingdom of Mercia and the Welsh kingdoms of Gwent and Powys. Hereford Cathedral originally dates back to the 670s, and the present building was begun in the 1070s; it contains the world-famous Mappa Mundi which dates to around 1300, during Edward II's lifetime.

Kenilworth Castle, Warwickshire: Edward is Forced to Abdicate

The mighty Kenilworth Castle in Warwickshire is strongly associated in many people's minds with Robert Dudley, earl of Leicester (c. 1532–88), and his hosting there of Queen Elizabeth I in 1575. This visit almost bankrupted the earl, and was a spectacle on a lavish and almost unprecedented scale. Kenilworth is also associated with Edward II's grandson John of Gaunt, second duke of Lancaster, who owned it from 1362 until his death in 1399 and who rebuilt the great hall, state apartments and several towers. Kenilworth was first built in the 1120s by the baron Geoffrey Clinton, treasurer of William the Conqueror's youngest son Henry I, and ultimately passed into royal hands, and King John oversaw a programme of extensive rebuilding and extending at Kenilworth, as was the case with several other royal castles during his reign. It was in John's reign that the extensive artificial lakes which were such a feature of medieval Kenilworth were first made; they surely inspired Gilbert 'the Red' de Clare when he built his own artificial lakes at Caerphilly a few decades later. John's son Henry III and his queen Eleanor of Provence stayed at Kenilworth in September 1238, around the time they must have conceived their first child, the future King Edward I, who was born on 17 June 1239. Henry gave Kenilworth to his brother-in-law Simon de Montfort, earl of Leicester, a French nobleman who had married his youngest sister Eleanor, in 1253.

The 1260s saw a series of conflicts between King Henry III, his son the future Edward I and his brother Richard of Cornwall against Simon de Montfort. The young Lord Edward defeated his uncle Montfort at the battle of Evesham in Worcestershire on 4 August 1265; Montfort and his eldest son Henry were killed, and the remainder of his family, including his widow, the king's sister Eleanor, fled abroad. Montfortian resistance to the king persisted in some quarters, however, and a number of them (including Montfort's second son Simon) held out at Kenilworth for many months. Henry III and his sons Edward and Edmund of Lancaster besieged the castle from 21 June until 13 December 1266, which may be the longest castle siege in English history. The garrison were finally compelled to surrender as they ran out of food, and the younger Simon de Montfort escaped to join his family overseas. Three days after the surrender, Henry III gave Kenilworth Castle to his younger son Edmund, then 21 years old.

Edmund of Lancaster, earl of Lancaster and Leicester, died on 5 June 1296, more than twenty years into the reign of his brother Edward I, and his heir was Thomas, eldest of his three sons. After Thomas's execution at Pontefract Castle in March 1322, Edward II kept most of the great Lancastrian inheritance of his uncle and cousin in his own hands, including Kenilworth. Subsequently, Edward often stayed at Kenilworth, including at Christmas 1323 and for much of March and April 1326; during the latter occasion, he hired a group of several dozen workmen to make a palisade in the park of Kenilworth, and invited a group of shipwrights from London to come and visit him. Thomas's brother and heir, Henry of Lancaster, unjustly disinherited of his stronghold of Kenilworth which was one of the most splendid castles in the kingdom, not surprisingly joined the invasion force of his niece Queen Isabella in early October 1326. She represented the best chance for Henry to regain his rightful inheritance from his cousin the king.

After Hugh Despenser the Younger's grotesque execution in Hereford, Henry of Lancaster took the captive king, treating him with every respect and courtesy, to Kenilworth Castle. They arrived there on, or a little before, 5 December 1326, and it was sixty years to the month since the castle had been given to Henry's father Edmund. Parliament was held in London in early 1327, and it was decided that the king must be made to abdicate his throne in favour of his 14-year-old son Edward of Windsor, whose reign as Edward III duly began on 25 January 1327. The news was taken to Edward II, now merely Sir Edward of Caernarfon, at Kenilworth. Various chroniclers say that he swooned or fainted on hearing the news, and the Westminster chronicle *Flores Historiarum* has Edward giving a dignified speech: 'I greatly lament that I have so utterly failed my people, but I could not be other than I am.'

Sir Edward of Caernarfon remained at Kenilworth Castle, while his wife and her allies ruled the kingdom in the name of his underage son, until 3 April 1327. We know little of his life there, but it is apparent that a group of his followers were attempting to free him and perhaps try to restore him to the throne, and it might even be that they attacked Kenilworth itself. Nothing came of this, as it was (with Caerphilly) the most impregnable castle in the country, but the danger of keeping a former king alive in the reign of his successor became clearer to the new rulers of the kingdom, Edward's wife Isabella and her allies including Roger Mortimer.

Kenilworth Castle is now looked after by English Heritage, and is open to the public daily except in winter, when it is generally only open at weekends, and is closed on 24, 25 and 26 December. It is just 5 miles from Warwick Castle and 18 miles from Birmingham.

Berkeley Castle, Gloucestershire: The Former King is Incarcerated

Remarkably, Berkeley Castle has belonged to the same family, the Berkeleys, since the twelfth century. It was originally built in 1067 shortly after the Norman Conquest by William the Conqueror's close friend and ally William FitzOsbern, and passed to the Berkeleys in the following century. Berkeley Castle, standing near the River Severn in Gloucestershire after it begins to widen out into the Bristol Channel, is located 20 miles from the great port of Bristol and the same distance from the cathedral city of Gloucester (where Edward II was buried in December 1327). The name is pronounced 'barkley' not 'burkley'.

Edward of Caernarfon was moved from Kenilworth to Berkeley Castle in April 1327, and his chief custodian there was Thomas, Lord Berkeley. Thomas was born around 1295, and married Roger Mortimer of Wigmore's eldest daughter Margaret in 1319, though she remained with her mother Joan for the time being as she was still too young to reside with her husband. Roger Mortimer and his son-in-law Thomas Berkeley, and Berkeley's father Maurice, joined the Contrariant rebellion of 1321/22. Thomas Berkeley was imprisoned between 1322 and 1326, and his wife Margaret was one of the three of Roger Mortimer's eight daughters incarcerated in a convent by Edward II in 1324, after Mortimer escaped from the Tower of London and fled abroad. Berkeley's father Maurice, Lord Berkeley, died in prison in 1326. Roger Mortimer's return to England at the head of an army with Edward II's Queen Isabella in September 1326 spelled the end of Edward and Hugh Despenser the Younger; Mortimer's daughter Margaret and son-in-law Thomas Berkeley were released and could finally resume – or begin – their married life.

At Kenilworth, Sir Edward of Caernarfon was under the care of his cousin Henry of Lancaster, who treated him with respect and honour, but Queen Isabella and Roger Mortimer did not trust Lancaster; his wealth, influence and prestige was a threat to them and to their continued rule, and they did their best to keep him away from the young king Edward III, even though he was now Edward's legal guardian. Mortimer and Isabella decided, therefore, to remove her husband from Lancaster's control and hand him over to men they could trust. These men were Mortimer's son-in-law Thomas Berkeley, Berkeley's brother-in-law Sir John Maltravers, a knight of Dorset, and Sir Thomas Gurney, a knight of Somerset.

Edward of Caernarfon was therefore taken from Kenilworth to Berkeley Castle, and it is apparent that those in charge of him did their best to lay false trails so that none of his supporters would know where he was. He was taken to Bristol, 20 miles in the opposite direction, and there is also evidence that he was in Corfe Castle in Dorset, 85 miles south of Berkeley, at some point in 1327. He, or more probably a decoy, may even have been taken to Chester much farther north, as some of the former king's supporters seem to have believed that he was there in early June 1327. Edward and his custodians spent one night at the priory of Llanthony Secunda in Gloucester en route to Berkeley Castle, and a man called Michael atte Hulle was a canon there. Michael and his nephew William were supporters of the deposed king, and almost certainly told their allies where Michael had seen Edward. A group of men were doing their utmost to free the deposed king, and had already tried to assault Kenilworth Castle earlier in 1327. The leader of the group was a Dominican friar and papal chaplain called Thomas Dunheved, aided by his brother Stephen, formerly lord of the manor of Dunchurch in Warwickshire. These men and their allies, including a few knights, clerics, sergeants-at-arms and former members of Edward's household, turned up in Chester in the early summer of 1327. They soon found out where the former king really was. One of the group was William Russell, parson of the church of Huntley in the Forest of

Dean, Gloucestershire, 22 miles from Berkeley. This would have made an ideally remote base as the gang laid their plans to free Edward.

Sometime in June or July 1327, the Dunheved gang launched an assault on Berkeley Castle. Almost nothing is known about the attack, but they were temporarily successful; Thomas, Lord Berkeley, told the chancellor of England on 27 July 1327 that the gang 'seized the father of our lord the king from our custody'. Presumably, though, they had to flee without Edward, or they managed to leave the castle with the former king, but he was captured shortly afterwards. The gang scattered; the friar Thomas Dunheved was captured 18 miles from his family home in Dunchurch, Warwickshire, and sent to prison in Pontefract Castle in Yorkshire, where he died. His brother Stephen was captured in London and sent to Newgate prison, though he escaped two years later and took part in a plot of Edward II's half-brother, the earl of Kent, to free Edward – by then supposedly long dead – in 1329/30. Another gang member, a parson called William Aylmer, was captured in Oxford in or before August 1327. Their attempt failed, but the Dunheved gang were not the only men trying to free Edward; Lord Berkeley wrote in his letter of 27 July 1327 that there was a plot in Bedfordshire and neighbouring counties, and in September a group of Welsh noblemen and knights made another attempt. Some of them were imprisoned in Caernarfon Castle (ironically enough, Edward's birthplace) and others fled to Scotland.

One later chronicler writing in the 1350s, Geoffrey le Baker, made up stories that Edward was tormented and abused while at Berkeley Castle, and that his jailers made him live above a deep pit where the rotting carcasses of animals were thrown in the hope that he would die of the stench and the contagion. These stories have far too often been repeated uncritically as though they are certainly true. They are not. Baker was not writing accurate history but a hagiography, a saint's life; he wished Edward to be canonised as a saint, and therefore made up tales about his patient forbearance of the suffering inflicted on him by lesser mortals, whom Baker memorably called the 'satraps of Satan'. All the evidence shows that in fact Edward was well treated at Berkeley Castle and had servants, good food and wine, and access to a chapel. His captors received the princely sum of £5 a day for his care; to put this in perspective, it was more than most people at the time earned in a year.

According to common report, Edward died at Berkeley Castle on 21 September 1327. Sir Thomas Gurney, one of his custodians, immediately set off to inform the young king of his father's death. Edward III, still not yet 15 years old, was in Lincoln, and sent a letter to his cousin John de Bohun, earl of Hereford, on 24 September stating that his 'very dear lord and father has been commanded to God' (the conventional and politely euphemistic way in the fourteenth century of saying that someone had died). Sir Edward of Caernarfon's body was moved the few miles from Berkeley Castle to St Peter's Abbey in Gloucester a month after death. For that month, it was guarded at Berkeley by only one man; a sergeant-at-arms called William Beaukaire, who just six months earlier had been pardoned as one of the garrison holding the late Hugh Despenser the Younger's stronghold of Caerphilly against Queen Isabella, with Despenser's son inside. Many of the men inside Caerphilly Castle with Beaukaire were involved in the plots to free Edward in 1327 and again in 1329/30, and it seems a little odd that he of all people was hired to guard Edward's dead body.

Contrary to common modern belief, it is virtually certain that Edward of Caernarfon was not murdered at Berkeley Castle by having a red-hot poker inserted inside him which burned out his insides. The story that the villagers of Berkeley could hear his screams as he was atrociously murdered is also an invention. No one involved in Edward's murder ever spoke about it publicly, the method of murder was never revealed, and chroniclers filled the gap with rumours or their own speculation. Edward was variously said to have died of natural causes, of illness, of grief, to have been suffocated or strangled, to have died in a fall, to have been poisoned, and so on. Some chroniclers just wrote that he had died at Berkeley without saying how, and the *Scalacronica* wrote that he died 'by what manner is not known, but God knows it'. The tale of the red-hot poker was a minority opinion related only by a couple of chroniclers distant in time and space from Berkeley, but because it is so lurid and disgusting and thus highly memorable, the tale became popular and by the end of the fourteenth century was being widely repeated as though it were certainly true. The dramatist Christopher Marlowe at the end of the sixteenth century also did much to spread the notion by including it in his play about Edward.

The story that Edward II was murdered at Berkeley Castle by means of a red-hot poker is still often repeated, not least by the tour guides at the castle, but there is really no reason to imagine that it is any more true than all the other speculation by fourteenth-century chroniclers, and the alternative – that Edward escaped from Berkeley and ultimately made his way to Italy – is even more intriguing. It is beyond doubt that many influential people in England and Wales in the late 1320s and early 1330s behaved as though they believed Edward was still alive.

Berkeley Castle is privately owned, but open to the public from around Easter until the end of October, from Sundays to Wednesdays, 11 am until 5 pm. Guided tours are available at no extra cost. It can be hired out for weddings – a dedicated website gives all the information – and for other private or corporate events. The twelfth-century keep where Edward of Caernarfon was probably held captive is the oldest part of the castle and was attacked during the Civil War in the 1640s; a breach made in the wall is still there. Inside the keep is the king's gallery, where you can peer through a window made in the thickness of the walls into the room where Edward II was supposedly held captive in 1327 (though the extensive rebuilding carried out on the castle over the last 700 years makes this notion uncertain). The kitchen, larders and buttery of Berkeley Castle date to the fourteenth century, as does the magnificent Great Hall. Just bear in mind that if the tour guides or your fellow visitors tell you the tale of the red-hot poker, take it with a very large pinch of salt.

Gloucester Cathedral, Gloucestershire: Edward's Burial Site

Until the Dissolution of the Monasteries ordered by Henry VIII in the sixteenth century, Gloucester Cathedral was an abbey dedicated to St Peter. The abbey was originally founded all the way back in around 678 by an Anglo-Saxon king called Osric, ruler of a small kingdom called the Hwicce, a sub-area of the much greater kingdom of Mercia and which covered parts of Gloucestershire, Worcestershire and Warwickshire, plus small parts of other counties. Osric was probably also the founder of Bath Abbey, and Gloucester Abbey's first abbess, Cyneburh, was probably his sister. In the mid-1000s the bishop of Worcester, Ealdred, founded a house of Benedictine monks on the site (the town of Gloucester lay within the diocese of Worcester until 1541). After the Norman Conquest of 1066, a Norman named Serlo became abbot of the house, and held the position from 1072 to 1104. Serlo is a very important figure in the history of the abbey as he rebuilt the abbey church which much later became Gloucester Cathedral. The church's foundation stone was laid in 1089 and the building was consecrated in 1100. William the Conqueror's eldest son Robert Curthose, formerly duke of Normandy and imprisoned for almost 30 years by his brother Henry I, was buried at the abbey in 1134.

Edward II's grandfather Henry III was crowned king of England at Gloucester Abbey on 28 October 1216. Henry was then only 9 years old, and his father King John had died suddenly at Newark Castle in Nottinghamshire a few days before with much of his kingdom under the control of Louis of France (the future King Louis VIII) who had invaded England at the invitation of much of the disgruntled English baronage. The town of Gloucester, in the south-west, was one of the few safe areas of the country for King John's son that were beyond the reach of Louis and his allies. Henry was crowned by the Italian papal legate to England, Guala Bicchieri, using a gold chaplet belonging to Henry's mother Isabelle of Angoulême, John's widow. The young king was crowned again, more conventionally, at Westminster Abbey a few years later.

After his (supposed) murder at Berkeley Castle on 21 September 1327, the body of the former King Edward II was moved the 20 miles to Gloucester on 21 October, in the custody of John Thoky, abbot of St Peter's Abbey in the town. After its removal to Gloucester, Edward's body was guarded by a group of men: knights called Robert Hastang or Hastings and Edmund Wasteneys, who received 6*s* 8*d* and 5*s* per day respectively for remaining with the body until 20 December, the day of Edward's funeral; two royal chaplains called Bernard Burgh and Richard Potesgrave (formerly Edward's chaplain and rector of Heckington in Lincolnshire, detailed elsewhere in this volume), at 3*s* each a day; two sergeants-at-arms called Bertrand de la More and John Enfield at 1*s* a day; and Andrew, a royal candle-maker. On 22 October, a royal clerk named Hugh Glanville or Glaunvyl was appointed to pay the wages paid to the men watching over Edward's body and any other expenses relating to the former king's death. He paid out £77 12*s*, and Edward II's funeral cost over £350 in total.

From 21 October to 20 December 1327, Edward's body lay in state at St Peter's Abbey in Gloucester. The sudden death of a deposed king was bound to arouse considerable public curiosity; Glanville's account refers to four great pieces of oak sawn into barriers by carpenters, designed to resist the pressure of crowding people pushing for a glimpse. Edward lay under a cover which was decorated with 800 gold leaves, with a wooden effigy of himself on top of it. This is the first time any such wooden effigy is known to have been used for a royal burial in England. The effigy, for which 40s was paid, was carved in the likeness of Edward, and was crowned with a copper gilt crown which cost 7s 3d. Edward's coronation robes from 1308 were sent from London, and used to dress the effigy. The whole lay on a hearse which was decorated at the four corners with great lions, made by a court painter called John de Eastwick; the lions wore mantles with the royal arms of England embroidered on them. Also on the hearse stood four images of the Evangelists, Saints Matthew, Mark, Luke and John, and outside it were images of eight angels carrying censers (containers for incense) and two more great lions.

Edward II's funeral took place at St Peter's on Sunday, 20 December 1327, though unfortunately not much is known about it. His son Edward III, who had turned 15 a month earlier, was certainly present – this was long before English royal etiquette began to demand that kings should not attend funerals – and so was Edward's widow Isabella. Roger Mortimer, ruling the kingdom as the dowager queen's chief counsellor, had himself a new black tunic made for the occasion, a piece of hypocrisy which the young king remembered three years later when he had Mortimer dragged to his execution wearing it. Edward II's niece Elizabeth de Burgh, née de Clare, was certainly there, and so was Edmund of Woodstock, earl of Kent, younger of Edward II's two half-brothers. Most probably, other relatives of the late king also attended, including Edward's other half-brother Thomas of Brotherton, earl of Norfolk, Edward and Isabella's three younger children John of Eltham, Eleanor of Woodstock and Joan of the Tower (now aged 11, 9 and 6), his cousin Henry, earl of Lancaster, his nephew-in-law John de Warenne, earl of Surrey, and as many of the English bishops and lords as were able to travel to rather remote Gloucester in winter. There is no list of attendees, or any indication as to what form the funeral took.

There was a movement in the fourteenth century to promote Edward II as a saint, however unlikely that might seem, which was enthusiastically promoted by his great-grandson Richard II. The king's tomb in the north ambulatory of St Peter's Abbey brought pilgrims to pray there and to hope for miracles, which brought the abbey considerable income. It is not entirely clear whether the abbey itself or Edward III paid for the tomb and effigy, but there is no doubt at all that the tomb was, and remains to this day, one of the great treasures of medieval England. A magnificent alabaster effigy of the king himself lies atop the tomb. Edward is depicted with long curly hair and a bushy beard, wears a crown, and holds his orb and sceptre. Two beautifully-carved angels sit on either side of his head, and his feet rest on a lion (one of the feet has broken off over the centuries). The effigy is somewhat married by graffiti carved on it before modern times. There is an ornamental limestone canopy, and until the Dissolution the whole would have been brightly painted and had candles burning around it. It must have been a truly impressive sight; indeed, it still is. It was restored in 2007/08.

When Henry VIII dissolved the religious houses of England and Wales between 1536 and 1542, he allowed those houses where his royal ancestors were buried to remain standing. Worcester Priory, where King John was buried in 1216, survived and became Worcester Cathedral. Westminster Abbey, site of so many royal burials, survived and is still Westminster Abbey. And St Peter's Abbey in Gloucester, where Edward II was buried, survived and became Gloucester Cathedral.

Gloucester Cathedral is open to visitors every day of the year, usually from 7.30 am until 6 pm, and four services are held on Sundays. Volunteers work on Sundays between 11.45 am and 2.45 pm and are available to answer any questions. The corridor scenes at Hogwarts were filmed in the cloisters of Gloucester Cathedral for the first, second and sixth Harry Potter films, and the BBC's Sherlock and Wolf Hall have also been filmed at the cathedral.

Tewkesbury Abbey, Gloucestershire: Burial Site of the Despensers

Just 10 miles from Gloucester, where Edward II was lain to rest in December 1327 – at least according to common story, whether true or not – lie the remains of Hugh Despenser the Younger and Despenser's wife Eleanor (1292–1337), Edward's eldest niece. Tewkesbury is a small historic town famous for a battle which took place there in 1471 between the forces of Edward IV and Henry VI's queen Margaret of Anjou, and its abbey is a particular highlight. Dedicated to the Virgin Mary, Tewkesbury Abbey was founded as a Benedictine monastery by the nobleman Robert FitzHamon in 1087, the year William the Conqueror died, and was consecrated in October 1121, during the reign of William's youngest son Henry I. Tradition has it, however, that an Anglo-Saxon abbey existed in Tewkesbury from about 715 onwards, and in the village of Deerhurst just 4 miles from Tewkesbury we find two religious buildings dating from Anglo-Saxon times: Odda's chapel, built in the 1050s, and St Mary's Priory Church, which contains much sculpture and carvings from the ninth and tenth centuries. The abbey church of Tewkesbury was saved from Henry VIII's commissioners in 1540 when the townspeople bought the building from them, at a cost of £453. They used the building as their parish church, and thus saved it for posterity. All other abbey buildings were, however, pulled down, and quarried for their stone and other materials.

In the thirteenth and fourteenth centuries, Tewkesbury Abbey was the mausoleum of the powerful and wealthy de Clare family, earls of Gloucester and Hertford, and among the Clares buried here are Edward II's decades-older brother-in-law Gilbert 'the Red' de Clare, earl of Gloucester and Hertford (1243–95), Gilbert's father Earl Richard (1222–62), and Gilbert's son and heir, Gilbert the younger (1291–1314), who was killed during his uncle Edward II's defeat at the battle of Bannockburn when he was 23. King Edward II himself visited Tewkesbury Abbey in January 1324 and laid an expensive cloth on his nephew's tomb. By then, the manor of Tewkesbury had passed to Gilbert's sister Eleanor and her husband Hugh Despenser the Younger, and they and several of their descendants would also be buried in the abbey.

On 19 October 1330, Edward III overthrew his mother Queen Isabella and her ally Roger Mortimer, and had Mortimer hanged at Tyburn on 29 November and Isabella confined for a time under comfortable house arrest. The young king gave permission on 15 December 1330 for the friends and family of Hugh Despenser the Younger to collect and bury his remains, whatever was left of them after four years' exposure to the elements. It is unclear exactly who collected Hugh's remains. Hugh was buried at Tewkesbury Abbey, which stood on Eleanor Despenser's lands, so whoever had collected Hugh's remains, Eleanor must have been responsible for burying him. She was by then married to her second husband William de la Zouche, lord of Ashby in Leicestershire, and bore him a son probably in 1330, but still took charge of her first husband's funeral. She chose to honour Hugh by interring him at her family's prestigious mausoleum, and given the climate of 1330, when Despenser was reviled as a dead and disgraced traitor, this perhaps was a rather defiant choice when she could equally have had him buried at a remote and obscure church somewhere else on her lands. Despenser's surviving sisters Alina Burnell, Isabella Hastings and Elizabeth Camoys, his nephew Philip Despenser, and some of his nine children, perhaps also attended his funeral (Queen Isabella, rather vindictively, had forced his middle three daughters to be veiled as nuns at three separate convents a few weeks after his execution).

Hugh Despenser's tomb was built in the ambulatory behind the high altar, and most peculiarly, the slab from the tomb of John Coles, abbot of Tewkesbury, who died in 1347, was placed on top of Despenser's. Perhaps this was intended only as a temporary arrangement – Hugh and Eleanor's eldest son was lord of Tewkesbury in 1347 and it hardly seems likely that anyone would have deliberately disrespected him and his family – but the slab remains there to this day. It is highly unusual for a man who suffered the traitor's death to have a burial site; traitors' bodies were cut into four pieces and displayed in public until they rotted away, when they were probably simply disposed of by being thrown into a river or onto a pile of rubbish. Hugh Despenser's tomb was vandalised during the Dissolution and afterwards, its fine decoration hacked away, but at Tewkesbury Abbey he lies still.

Despenser's widow Eleanor de Clare died in June 1337 and was also buried at Tewkesbury Abbey, though the exact location of her grave within the abbey church is not known. Their eldest son and heir Hugh, or 'Huchon', succeeded as lord of Glamorgan, and died in February 1349 at the age of 40, perhaps of the Black Death which was then ravaging England. His magnificent effigy, lying next to that of his wife Elizabeth Montacute (d. 1359), daughter of the earl of Salisbury, is still there behind the high altar, in the same position as his father Hugh's on the other side of the altar. Huchon's effigy wears armour of the mid-fourteenth century, and Elizabeth is depicted wearing a square head-dress which was surely the height of contemporary fashion.

The town of Tewkesbury stands on the confluence of the rivers Severn and Avon, the same River Avon that flows through Stratford-on-Avon. A pub in the town, the Black Bear, is said to be the oldest pub in Gloucestershire and dates back to 1308, early in Edward II's reign, and as well as the abbey, the town boasts many other medieval and Tudor buildings.

Corfe Castle, Dorset: Edward is Incarcerated

The history of a fortified location at Corfe in Dorset dates back a remarkably long time. On 18 March 978, the king of England, Edward the Martyr, was murdered at Corfe supposedly on the orders of his stepmother so that her son, his half-brother Aethelred, could succeed to the throne in his place. It was William the Conqueror (r. 1066–87), however, who turned Corfe into a mighty fortification, and his youngest son Henry I (r. 1100–35) built the great stone keep in 1105. Edward II's great-grandfather King John spent much time at Corfe and spent a lot of money renovating it, and his son Henry III, Edward's grandfather, spent far more. Edward I completed Corfe by building the stone gatehouse.

Corfe Castle's history has not always been a happy one. As well as the murder of Edward the Martyr on (or near) the site of the present castle in 978, it became the prison of one Eleanor of Brittany in, or soon after, 1203. Eleanor was the only daughter of King John's late older brother Geoffrey, duke of Brittany, and had a claim to the throne which John did not wish her to pass on to a husband or son, so he kept her in confinement all her life. Her 16-year-old younger brother Arthur (Duke Geoffrey's posthumous son) disappeared in 1203, almost certainly murdered on John's orders as he was a threat to John's possession of the English throne. One of the most notorious incidents of John's turbulent reign occurred either at Corfe or at Windsor, when the king had the noblewoman Maude de Braose and her son starved to death in a dungeon after her husband quarrelled with John, and Maude stated publicly that John had had his own nephew, Arthur of Brittany, murdered. By Edward II's time in the early fourteenth century, Corfe had become a royal prison, and Edward used it to incarcerate some of the Contrariants in 1321/22. One of them, Sir Robert Walkfare, escaped from Corfe in, or before, 1326 by killing a porter named William le Foulere, and was pardoned for the break-out and for the murder in 1327 at the start of Edward III's reign. Edward II himself never visited Corfe during his reign, though ordered an inquisition on it in January 1326 to determine what repairs were needed. The inquisition reveals that Corfe had a tower called 'Cockayne', a 'high tower with chambers and garderobes', a 'long hall' and a 'queen's hall' with its own porch. There was a gate called 'Middelghete' or 'middle gate' in fourteenth-century English, a 'great outside gate' with a bridge leading to it, and a third gate containing a chapel dedicated to the Virgin Mary.

Edward was forced to abdicate his throne to his teenage son Edward III in January 1327, and a few weeks later was sent from captivity at Kenilworth Castle in Warwickshire to Berkeley Castle in Gloucestershire. Supposedly, he was murdered at Berkeley on 21 September 1327, and officially, he was never incarcerated at Corfe Castle and never even went near the place. There is, however, a curiously large amount of evidence which places him at the castle at some point in 1327. The well-informed chronicler Adam Murimuth, who was a royal clerk and close to the centre of government affairs – and in the south-west of England in 1327 – wrote that Edward's captors took him to Corfe and elsewhere before they took him to Berkeley so that it could not be ascertained where he was (a sensible precaution, as several of Edward's followers were trying their best to free him from captivity and perhaps restore him to his lost throne). The author of the Middle English *Brut* chronicle thought that Edward was murdered at Corfe in September 1327, a version of the French *Brut* chronicle wrote that he was taken from Kenilworth to Corfe, and the author of an anonymous chronicle from Flanders also wrote that Edward was sent to Corfe after his capture in South Wales in November 1326. This last point is certainly incorrect, but does reveal the strong association of the deposed Edward II with Corfe Castle and the way some chroniclers were convinced he was imprisoned there. As mentioned previously, there is a record of Edward's captors taking him from Kenilworth Castle to the city of Bristol before eventually taking him to Berkeley; Bristol is 20 miles from Berkeley, in the opposite direction from Kenilworth in Warwickshire, so it does seem as though they were deliberately planting false trails and perhaps also took him to Corfe for a similar purpose. Corfe is about 85 miles south of Berkeley.

Sometime a little before 29 September 1327, Edward of Caernarfon's joint custodian at Berkeley Castle, Sir John Maltravers, received letters from the other custodian, Thomas Berkeley, at Corfe Castle. At the same time, Maltravers was paid £258 for his 'services to the king's [Edward III's] father in Dorset'. Although Edward of Caernarfon was supposedly murdered at Berkeley Castle on 21 September 1327, had he perhaps been secretly sent to Corfe instead? There is more evidence which places him there after his supposed death in September 1327. The Fieschi Letter was written c. 1336/38 by an Italian notary of the pope called Manuele Fieschi, a nobleman by birth and later Bishop of Vercelli near Milan. In his letter, Fieschi informed Edward III in detail how his father, Edward II, had escaped from Berkeley Castle by killing a porter – as Robert Walkfare had done at Corfe in, or before, 1326 – and made his way to Corfe Castle, where he lived for eighteen months. Edward, the Fieschi Letter ran, subsequently made his way to Ireland, then after the execution of Roger Mortimer in late 1330, to Flanders, through France, to visit Pope John XXII in Avignon, to Cologne, and on to Milan, and then to a hermitage south of Milan which can be identified as Sant'Alberto di Butrio.

William Melton, archbishop of York, was a close friend and ally of Edward II who was one of the few men who supported the king in 1326/27. The archbishop was indicted before King's Bench in 1330 after he wrote a letter to the Mayor of London in January that year asserting that Edward II was still alive, and told Edward's Scottish friend the earl of Mar that Edward was alive (Mar promised to bring an enormous force of men to England to secure Edward's release, and archbishop Melton was thus accused of treason for inviting a foreign army to England). An informer told the King's Bench that Melton had received a messenger in October 1329, telling him that Edward II was 'alive and in good health in the prison of Corfe Castle'. Edward's half-brother Edmund of Woodstock, earl of Kent, also believed in 1329/30 that Edward was still alive, and tried to free him from captivity. Kent was arrested on 13 March 1330, and three days later made a full confession about his plot and named some of his followers. The plan was to take Edward along the coast to the earl's castle at Arundel in Sussex, by boat and ship. Kent did not state where he believed his half-brother to be hiding or imprisoned, but given the wealth of evidence placing Edward II at Corfe Castle in and after 1327, Kent probably also believed this. The notion that Edward survived his supposed murder and was secretly alive for years afterwards might seem laughably absurd, but many influential men in 1329/30 strongly believed that he was not dead at all, even his own half-brother who had attended his funeral in Gloucester. Kent was beheaded in March 1330 for the 'crime' of trying to free a dead man from captivity, and many of his followers were arrested and imprisoned, and their lands and goods were confiscated. Others fled abroad.

Corfe Castle was attacked by parliamentarians in 1646 during the Civil War and was left partly in ruins, but is still spectacular and picturesque; it stands on a hill and commands exceptional views. It is open daily except Christmas Day and Boxing Day, and is looked after by the National Trust.

Nottingham Castle, Nottinghamshire: Edward's Son Overthrows his Mother

From early 1327 until October 1330, Edward II's queen Isabella of France ruled England in the name of her underage son Edward III. She had not been appointed regent, or even as a member of the council appointed to govern until the teenage king reached his majority, but that did not stop her, and she and her chief counsellor Roger Mortimer appropriated royal power and used it to grant themselves lands and money to which they were not entitled. Isabella gave herself the largest income which anyone in England (except the kings) received throughout the entire Middle Ages, Mortimer bestowed the brand-new and grandiose earldom of March on himself in October 1328, and they made a peace settlement with Scotland to which Isabella's son, the young king, was fundamentally opposed but could not prevent. It is often stated nowadays that Isabella and Roger Mortimer were lovers and had fallen passionately in love, and this is certainly not impossible, though some fourteenth-century chroniclers merely call Mortimer Isabella's 'chief counsellor', or even just 'of her faction', and seem unaware of any love affair. The Lanercost chronicler in the far north of England wrote in the 1340s that he had heard rumours of a 'liaison' between them, and royal clerk Adam Murimuth, who knew the two well, wrote of their 'familiarity', and had said exactly the same thing about Edward II and Piers Gaveston. A later chronicler, Jean Froissart, claimed that Isabella was pregnant at the time of their downfall in October 1330, but no English chronicler even hints at this, and Froissart was not born until c. 1337 and only arrived in England in the early 1360s after Isabella's death. It is possible that Isabella and Roger Mortimer were lovers, though if so they did not, contrary to another popular modern belief, flaunt their relationship or live together openly.

Whatever went on in private between the queen mother and the baron, by 1330 they had bankrupted the kingdom and Mortimer began to treat Edward III with increasing disrespect, rudely remaining seated in his presence and even walking ahead of him. The young king had had enough. On 15 June 1330, his 16-year-old queen Philippa of Hainault gave birth to their son Edward of Woodstock, and securing the succession to his throne gave Edward III the confidence to act. The problem was, he could not raise an army against his mother and her chief counsellor without them noticing, and, to his utter fury, they had placed spies in his household; he later referred to himself as being 'like a man living in custody'. Edward spent many months secretly gathering a group of loyal young knights around him, and sometime in 1329 or early 1330 managed to send his close friend Sir William Montacute to Pope John XXII in Avignon to gain his support.

On 19 October 1330, Edward III and twenty or so young knights burst into the room at Nottingham Castle where Queen Isabella was holding a meeting with Mortimer and their few remaining allies, including Mortimer's son Geoffrey and the Bishop of Lincoln. The king had gained access to the room by using a secret tunnel into the castle. He had Mortimer arrested, though Queen Isabella supposedly cried out to the king: 'Fair son, have pity on gentle Mortimer' ('gentle' in the medieval sense meant 'of noble birth' and was not a statement on Mortimer's character). The self-important earl of March was taken to imprisonment at the Tower of London, and hanged at Tyburn near London on 29 November 1330 on charges of appropriating royal power which did not belong to him. Queen Isabella was temporarily held under house arrest, and was made to give up her vast income and the lands she had taken from others.

The years from January 1327 to October 1330, the first few years of Edward III's reign, belong more fittingly to the reign of Edward II rather than that of his son. The regime of Edward II's wife Isabella proved no better than the one it replaced, and the people of England realised they had exchanged the rule of the king and a ruthless, greedy baron (Hugh Despenser the Younger), for that of the queen and a ruthless, greedy baron (Roger Mortimer). Even men who had played an important role in the downfall of Edward II in 1326/27 turned against the new regime by late 1328, and there were several rebellions against the queen mother and Mortimer's regime which failed. By the autumn of 1330, it was apparent that any further significant opposition to the pair had to come from the young king himself, and he rose to the challenge. After 19 October 1330 – still not quite 18 years old (he was born on 13 November 1312) – he began to rule his kingdom himself, and proved to be an excellent ruler and especially an excellent war leader. He reigned until his death in June 1377. As Edward III and Queen Philippa's eldest son Edward of Woodstock, Prince of Wales, died a year before his father, Edward III was succeeded by his 10-year-old grandson Richard II. As a king, Richard II was cast far more in the mould of his great-grandfather Edward II than his grandfather, and suffered the same fate of deposition in 1399. Richard was well aware of his and Edward's similarities, and spent much of his reign trying unsuccessfully to persuade the pope to canonise Edward as a saint.

Nottingham Castle stands on a promontory called Castle Rock, and was built soon after the Norman Conquest. The original medieval castle was mostly demolished in the seventeenth century, and a seventeenth-century ducal mansion converted into a museum in 1878 stands on the site. Mortimer's Hole, a long tunnel cut through the rock and traditionally said to be Edward III's way into the castle to arrest Roger Mortimer in October 1330, can still be visited and is part of a labyrinth of tunnels and caves cut into the rock. Some of the caves date back to medieval times.

Castle Rising, Norfolk: Favourite Residence of Edward's Widow

Isabella of France, the dowager queen, was still only 35 years old at the end of 1330 when her son Edward III overthrew her and her chief ally Roger Mortimer, and she lived for another twenty-eight years. It is often stated that she went insane after her son executed her beloved Roger Mortimer, though there is no evidence for this. It is true that the dowager queen was temporarily deprived of her freedom of movement, but she was very soon released, and spent the remaining years of her life travelling between her estates, buying jewels, entertaining numerous visitors, and listening to musicians; in short living the entirely conventional life of a dowager queen. It is emphatically not the case that Isabella was imprisoned at Castle Rising in Norfolk by her son, as a popular modern narrative insists. She did spend much time there, but because it was her favourite residence rather than because she was not permitted to leave, and she died at Hertford Castle on 22 August 1358. Another popular, but inaccurate,modern tale states that Isabella was buried next to her long-dead but never forgotten lover Roger Mortimer. Isabella was buried at the Greyfriars church in London in late November 1358; Mortimer had not been buried there, but at the Greyfriars in Coventry, and his body may have been moved to Wigmore in Herefordshire, his family's main seat. Isabella's aunt Marguerite of France, the second wife of Edward I and stepmother of Edward II, had been buried at the Greyfriars in London in 1318, and four years after Isabella's death, her younger daughter, Queen Joan of

Scotland, was also buried there. Isabella was interred with the clothes she had worn at her wedding to Edward II half a century previously, and according to a later tradition, with her husband's heart laid in a vessel on her chest (though this was not recorded until the sixteenth century and may not be accurate). The Greyfriars church in London was destroyed in the Great Fire in 1666, rebuilt but then destroyed again during the Blitz in 1940/41, and Isabella's tomb is therefore lost.

Isabella's preferred residence for many years, Castle Rising, was built in and after 1138 by William d'Albini, earl of Arundel (d. 1176), for his wife Adeliza of Louvain (d. 1151), widow of King Henry I (r. 1100–35). It lies 5 miles from King's Lynn, and in the Middle Ages would have been reached by boat. It is surrounded by massive earthworks, the whole area covers at least 12 acres, and the keep is one of the largest, best preserved and most ornate in the country. A great hall spanned two floors of the three floors of the keep, and in the fourteenth century a deer park lay nearby. Although the castle looks massive, mighty and domineering, it does not appear to have been built with the intention of defending anything (such as an important road or river crossing, or a port) and therefore was apparently built simply as a home and to provide a convenient base for the large hunting park nearby. After Isabella of France's death in August 1358, Castle Rising passed to her eldest grandson Edward of Woodstock, Prince of Wales (1330–76). It is now managed by English Heritage, and Castle Acre Priory nearby is also worth a visit. The castle is open most days of the year, except Christmas Eve, Christmas Day and Boxing Day, though it might be closed one or two days of the week in winter.

Afterword

There are many sites in Britain strongly associated with Edward II, and some which he himself would still recognise if he could travel forward 700 years. Further afield, for readers wishing to trace Edward's footsteps to locations beyond Britain, there are other sites in France, Spain, Germany and Italy also associated with the king. Parts of northern France have an especially strong connection to Edward II; he married Isabella of France in the town of Boulogne-sur-Mer in the department of Pas-de-Calais (20 miles from the port of Calais) on 25 January 1308, in a magnificent ceremony attended by Isabella's father Philip IV of France, her brother Louis, king of Navarre, and many other European royals. Edward II inherited the northern French county of Ponthieu from his mother Leonor of Castile and his grandmother Jeanne of Ponthieu (c. 1217/20–79), queen of Castile and Leon; both women were countesses of Ponthieu in their own right. Ponthieu no longer exists on the political map of France, but covered much of the area of the modern departments of Somme and Pas-de-Calais, and its chief towns were Abbeville and Montreuil-sur-Mer. Edward II himself visited the area in 1308, 1312, 1313 and 1320, and his son Edward III won a great victory over the French at the battle of Crécy on 26 August 1346 near a town which is still called Crécy-en-Ponthieu. Some of the great battles of the First World War, notably the Battle of the Somme in 1916, took place in an area of France which once belonged to Edward II.

Edward, as well as being count of Ponthieu, was duke of Aquitaine in southern France from 1306 to 1327, a territory he inherited from his father Edward I and ultimately from his great-great-grandmother Eleanor of Aquitaine (c. 1124–1204), queen of France and England. Edward I gave Edward the island of Oléron on the west coast of France, south of

La Rochelle, at the same time as he made his son duke of Aquitaine in May 1306, and Oléron is now a popular tourist destination, mostly with French visitors (foreigners tend to head for nearby Île de Ré). Although Edward never set foot in the south of France in person, one chronicler claimed it was the land which he loved the best. Piers Gaveston's family originally came from, and were named after, the village of Gabaston, in the foothills of the Pyrenees not far from the Spanish border. Gabaston is located in the modern department of Pyrénées-Atlantiques and 20 miles from the great pilgrim destination of Lourdes. Edward II's brother Alfonso, who died at the age of 10 in August 1284 when Edward was 4 months old, was born in the town of Bayonne near Biarritz in November 1273, and Edward's great-grandson Richard II was born in Bordeaux in January 1367 while his father, Edward's grandson the Prince of Wales and Aquitaine, was ruling the duchy.

There are several places in Spain associated with Edward II's family. Many of his close relatives, including his grandfather King Fernando III of Castile and Leon and his uncle King Alfonso X, are buried in Seville Cathedral in southern Spain, the second-largest church in Europe after St Peter's in Rome. Fernando III died in Seville in May 1252. He was canonised as a saint of the Catholic Church in 1671 and is now patron saint of the city of Seville; his feast day is 30 May, the date of his death in 1252. There is also a valley in California named after Edward II's grandfather, the San Fernando Valley. Edward's uncle Don Felipe was archbishop of Seville, and another uncle, Don Sancho, was archbishop of Toledo, 50 miles south of Madrid in central Spain. Edward's mother Leonor of Castile may have been born in Valladolid, the largest city in north-western Spain, in late 1241, and was surely present when her father Fernando rode into Seville in triumph when she was 7 years old in December 1248, having captured the city from its Muslim rulers. Leonor married Edward II's father in 1254 at the Abbey of Santa Maria la Real de Las Huelgas just outside Burgos, northern Spain, which still exists and is still a working monastery. It was founded in 1187 by Edward II's great-great-grandparents Alfonso VIII (1155–1214) and Eleanor of England (1162–1214), king and queen of Castile. It is open to the public, and stands little more than a mile from the medieval cathedral of Burgos.

Officially, Edward died at Berkeley Castle, Gloucestershire, on 21 September 1327, but there is much evidence that he survived for years past that date. According to the Fieschi Letter of the 1330s, addressed to

Edward's son Edward III by an Italian nobleman, papal notary and later bishop of Vercelli called Manuele Fieschi, Edward fled from Berkeley to Corfe Castle in Dorset, then went to Ireland (where exactly is not stated). After the execution of Roger Mortimer in November 1330, says the Fieschi Letter, Edward travelled to the continent and walked all the way through France to visit Pope John XXII in Avignon for fifteen days. He subsequently passed through the German city of Cologne, so Fieschi claimed, where he worshipped at the shrine of the Three Kings in Cologne Cathedral. The 'Three Kings' are the Magi or Wise Men of the Gospels who brought gifts of gold, frankincense and myrrh to the infant Jesus Christ, and their bodily remains were allegedly originally buried at the church of Sant'Eustorgio in Milan. The German emperor Frederick Barbarossa removed them to Cologne when he invaded and looted Milan in 1162. A magnificent golden shrine made in 1191 to house the remains of the Magi can be seen to this day in Cologne Cathedral.

After visiting Cologne, says the Fieschi Letter, Edward made his way south through Germany and over the Alps to Milan, and ended up living for several years at a hermitage called Sant'Alberto di Butrio about 60 miles south of Milan. This hermitage, high in the hills above the Staffora Valley and about 3 miles from the castle of Oramala, still exists and is still a working community, and can be visited daily. It would seem oddly appropriate if Edward II, the most unconventional of English kings and one who loved the outdoors and hard physical exercise, escaped from England and ended his days secretly living in a hermitage, participating in the kind of activities he had always enjoyed but for which he had always been condemned.

Further Reading

My biographies of Edward II, his queen Isabella of France, and his powerful chamberlain Hugh Despenser the Younger: *Edward II: The Unconventional King* (2014), *Isabella of France: The Rebel Queen* (2016), and *Hugh Despenser the Younger and Edward II: Downfall of a King's Favourite* (2018).

My investigation into Edward's murder in 1327, or his possible survival years past that date: *Long Live the King: The Mysterious Fate of Edward II* (2017).

Edward II by Seymour Phillips (2010), a magisterial, exhaustive yet highly readable biography in the excellent Yale English Monarchs series. W. M. Ormrod's *Edward III* (2011) is the successor volume in the same series.

King Edward II: His Life, His Reign, and Its Aftermath, 1284–1330 (2003) by Roy Martin Haines: highly academic and extremely thorough.

Edward II The Man: A Doomed Inheritance by Stephen Spinks (2017): a sympathetic and very readable look at Edward's life and reign.

Edward II: The Terrors of Kingship by Christopher Given-Wilson (2016): a short (under 150 pages) introduction to Edward and his reign, in the Penguin Monarchs series. Equally short biographies of Edward's father Edward I by Andy King (2017) and his son Edward III by Jonathan Sumption (2016) are also available in the same series.

Index